The Fall of Adam and Other Works

By John Greene

The Fall of Adam and Other Works
By John Greene

Edited and updated by C. Matthew McMahon and Therese B. McMahon
Transcribed by Daniel Kok

Copyright © 2013 by Puritan Publications and A Puritan's Mind

Some language and grammar has been updated from the original manuscript. Any change in wording or punctuation has not changed the intent or meaning of the original author(s), and has been made to aid the modern reader.

Published by Puritan Publications
A Ministry of A Puritan's Mind
4101 Coral Tree Circle #214
Coconut Creek, FL 33073
www.puritanshop.com
www.apuritansmind.com
www.puritanpublications.com

This Print Edition, 2013
Electronic Edition, 2013
Manufactured in the United States of America

ISBN: 978-1-62663-033-8
eISBN: 978-1-62663-032-1

*Cover: Adam's Expulsion from the Garden, by Masaccio (1401-1428), painter of frescoes during the early Italian Renaissance.*

# TABLE OF CONTENTS

# MEET JOHN GREENE

John Greene (d. 1660), was Pastor of Pencombe, a Presbyterian and Reformed minister, and a member of the Assembly of Divines at Westminster. Not much is known about him, except for the *following:*

He received a liberal education, and was eminently learned and pious. He was for sometime pastor of Pencombe, in the county of Hereford; and he carefully fed his people with knowledge, and warned them of danger. He was much against the unhallowed book of sports. The appearance of that declaration was a great grievance to him, and he freely expressed his sentiments on the subject. In his sermon from Nehemiah 1:3-4, which he preached to the house of commons, he says, "they were my meditations upon the coming forth of that book for that sinful liberty on the Lord's Day, (and I did not forbear to express them) when I too often heard, in neighboring parishes, drums beating up for a marrice or a may-pole on that day, we had just cause to fear, lest the lord should punish that sin, with beating up drums for a march on that day and the lord," (Life and Writings of John Greene, 365). He continued, "Hath these brought our fears upon us. How many marclies have been on that day, since the beginning of these wars? I have long thought it one of the highest provoking sins of this land." Mr. Greene seems, with others, to have considered the Lord of hosts, as punishing that general and leading sin, the heaven-daring profanation of the Lord's Day, by the mournful battle at Kineton, or Edgehill, on that day. He adds, "But I hope those many ordinances for suppressing this profaneness will be a good means, through God's mercy, to quench our unnatural flames, if to good laws, which are the life of a state, be added careful execution, which is the life of laws."

In 1643, Mr. Greene was chosen one of the Assembly of Divines at Westminster; and he is in Mr. Neal's list marked as giving constant attendance. He often preached to the parliament. According to Dr. Calamy, he died in the very week that he was preparing to quit his living on the Bartholomew Act, in 1660.

*His works:*

Mr. Greene wrote and published a sermon which is entitled, "Nehemiah's tears and prayers for Judah's affliction, and the ruins and repair of Jerusalem." This sermon was preached from Neh. 1:3-4, in the church of Margaret, Westminster, before the house of commons, upon the day of their monthly humiliation. He also published, "The First Man, or, A Short Discourse of Adam's State," as well as a sermon on, "The Church's Duty for Received Mercies," on 1 Samuel 12:24,

"Only fear the Lord, and serve him in truth, with all your heart; for consider what great things he hath done for you."

Taken in part from James Reid's work, "Memoirs of the Lives and Writings of Those Eminent Divines..." (Paisley: Steven and Andrew Young, 1811), page 364, and also Thomas Smith's work, "Select Memoirs of the Scottish and English Divines" (Puritan Publications: Coconut Creek, 2012), page 571.

# IMPRIMATUR: SERMON 1

*Die Mercurij* 24<sup>th</sup>. February, 1646.

Ordered by the Commons Assembled in Parliament, that Sir *Robert Harley* does from this House give thanks to Master Greene, for the great pains he took in his sermon preached on this day at *Margaret's Westminster* before the House of Commons; and that he desires him to print his sermon: in which, he is to have the same privilege in its printing, as others in the some way usually have had.

*H. Elsing Cler. Parl. D. Com.*

---

I do appoint Philemon Stephens to print my sermon.

## JOHN GREENE

# [ORIGINAL TITLE PAGE]

# The
# CHURCH'S
## Duty,
## for received Mercies.

Discovered in a SERMON Preached
Before the Honorable House
OF
# COMMONS:

At *Margaret's Westminster*, Feb. 24.
1646. being the day of the solemn
Monthly FAST.

---

By JOHN GREENE Minister of GOD'S Word,
and a member of the Assembly of DIVINES.

---

DEUTERONOMY 4:7. *For what Nation is so great, who hath God so nigh unto them, as the Lord our God is in all things that we call upon him for.*

VERSES 10, 12. *And now Israel what doth the Lord thy God require of thee, but to fear the Lord thy God, to walk in all his ways, and to love him, and to serve the Lord thy God with all thy heart, and with all thy soul.*

---

*LONDON,*
Printed by F.B. for Philemon Stephens, and are to be sold at
his shop at the gilded Lion in Paul's Church-yard. 1647.

# INTRODUCTION

## To the Honorable House

## OF

# COMMONS,

## Now Assembled in Parliament

There is not a greater enriching act of the soul, or of greater prevalence to provoke to duty, then the soul's reflection on itself by meditation. It is of utmost seriousness.[1] There is no greater manner in working this way, then the distinct consideration of what God has been to us, what we are to God, what we have received from him, and what our returns to him should be. David in one psalm calls up his soul to this duty, "Bless the Lord O my soul, and forget not all his benefits," (Psalm 103:2). In another he consults with himself, *how* he may do it, "what shall I render unto the Lord, for all his benefits towards me?" (Psalm 116:12). We have examples in nature leading us by the way they accomplish this duty. First, by what they are mutually to each other; what water the earth receives from the sea in small springs, it returns in great rivers;

---

[1] *Meditation mentis distatio.*

what vapours and exhalations the celestial bodies draw up from the earth, they send down (though sometimes in storms) yet ordinarily in refreshing dews and fruitful showers. Secondly, by what they are to man; does not the vineyard we plant yield us fruit? The flock we feed afford us milk? (1 Corinthians 9:7). The ground we manure and till, "give seed to the sower, and bread to the eater?" (Isaiah 55:10). Thirdly, by what they are to God; do not, "the heavens declare the glory of God?" (Psalm 19:1). Does not that which may seem most unruly, "stormy wind fulfill his word?" (Psalm 148:8). It was a divine saying of that heathenish Philosopher Epictetus[2], admiring the singing of birds, *si luscinia essem, etc.* If I had been made a nightingale, I should have sung like a nightingale; now I am made a man, a reasonable creature, shall I not praise and serve God in that station in which he has set me? Origin conceived, that one of the foulest and most shameful things that the creatures shall lay to man's charge at the day of judgement, is, that all other creatures from the creation have been obedient to God without the least digression; only man (for whose service), have proved rebellious. To quicken us to that service, which God in our places requires, was the principal drift of my weak meditations, so unworthy your ear, as I do not know how they may endure your eye; of which though I may say, as is reported of Malcotius, a governor of

---

[2] *Alsted. Theol. nat.*

the Turks under Mahommed the great (as it was also of Augustus), that the majesty of his countenance, with the resplendent beams issuing from his eyes, was of such piercing brightness, that no man was able with an unmoved and fixed eye, long to behold the same. Yet that benign aspect and favourable acceptance which those find whom you call out to your service, your present commands also requiring it, give encouragement to tender my poor endeavours to the public view; by which if any more people provoked to render to God, according to all that good they have received from God, let all the glory be the Lord's, who works when, and where, and by whom he pleases. For whose merciful assistance, direction and blessing in and on your pious consultations and resolutions, are and shall be the constant and continued prayers of,

The unworthiest of those devoted to Your service,
JOHN GREENE.

# THE CHURCH'S DUTY FOR RECEIVED MERCIES

*in a sermon preached before the Honorable House of Commons February, 24, 1647.*

1 Samuel 12:24, "Only fear the Lord, and serve him in truth, with all your heart; for consider what great things he hath done for you."

Sermons formerly in this place on these days were used much for stirring up to service in the cause of God, religion and the kingdom. The Lord having comfortably and successfully worked that, I conceive such texts will not now be thought unreasonable, which may afford matters of incitement to work our hearts to the service of God. To this the words read chiefly drive, being part of Samuel's counsel to the people of Israel (1 Samuel 8:7), who though rejected by them yet continues his love to them (others neglect of us, may not excuse our failings to them). Their request in a former verse of this chapter to Samuel was (verse 19), that "he would pray for them." Samuel does more, (religious hearts in duties of piety will strive rather to out go the desires of others, than fall short). He does not only, in the verse before the text, profess his readiness to pray for them, but he also cares to teach them, pray for pardon of their errors past, and set them in a way to prevent miscarriage for the time to come. And this way is worth listening to; it is first, a good way, that is interpreters say, *much for your good*, a prosperous way (Joshua 1:8), and the Hebrew word טובה will bear this sense. Secondly, a right way, which if we keep, we have no fear of being misled.

What this good and right way is, he shows in the words we read, "Fear the Lord and serve him, *etc.*" (Joshua 24:14). The paths are two, though Masius in the place of Joshua offers to bring 600 places in the Old Testament, in which the fear and service of God are all the same, however I shall balk the first, and endeavour to lead you into the second.

In the discovery of this, I shall *consider*,

First, the *duty* enjoined, "Serve the Lord."

Secondly, the *conditions* in this service; and these two, the one respecting the sincerity of our service, it must be, "in truth;" the other the *completeness* of it, and the *cheerfulness* in it, "with all the heart."

Thirdly, the reason enforcing the duty, "for consider what great things he hath done for you."

In the enlarging of the *duty*, I shall first show what it is to serve God. Secondly, that it is a duty which God requires. Thirdly, what cause there is why we should yield to it.

For the first, every service (if such as it ought) implies two duties; subjection, and obedience to be under the command of another, and to do his commands; in reference to these servants are said, "to be under the yoke," (1 Timothy 6:1), servants may not do what they wish, but are at their master's disposing; we shall find them both joined in that people's resolution, "The Lord our God will we serve, and his voice will we obey," (Joshua 24:24); so in a former verse of this Chapter, "if ye will serve the Lord and obey his voice," (Joshua 24:14). To serve God then is both to profess our subjection to him as our chiefest Lord, and also to endeavour to make good our obedience unto all his commands, and that accomplished well, for note all religious worship due to God, "Thou shalt worship the Lord thy God, and him only shalt thou serve," (Matthew 4:10), as for all particular duties which in our several relations God requires of us. Therefore, magistrates serving God in their places, are said, "to judge not for man but for God," (2 Chronicles 19:6), and the judgement given is called, "God's judgement," (Deuteronomy 1:17).

Ministers performing the work of the ministry, are called the, "servants of God and of Christ;" so Paul, Peter, and Jude (Titus 1:1; 2 Peter 1:1; Jude 1) are called this.

Commanders in war appearing in God's cause against his enemies, are said to fight God's battles; so Saul and Abigail say to David, "my Lord fighteth the Battles of the Lord," (1 Samuel 18:17, 25, 28).

Servants in their faithful service to their masters are called, "the servants of Christ," (Ephesians 6:6), are said, "to do the will of God, to serve the Lord Christ," (Colossians 3:22-24).

That to serve God is a duty required, the Scripture is so full, and a truth so well known, that I shall only commend it to you.

First, Joshua's charge to the people a little before his death is this, "Now therefore fear the Lord and serve him," (Joshua 24:14, 15, 18, 24).

Secondly, his own resolution, "I and my household will serve the Lord."

Thirdly, the peoples willing profession, "we also will serve the Lord, for he is our God."

For the third, there are two main encouragements to a service; the person whom we are to serve, and the service itself; and can there be any tie or engagement to any person, anything desirable in any service, which is not to be found in the Lord our Master in Heaven, and in his service?

Will he first serve him that made us? And every workman expects either the use or benefit of his workmanship; hear the Psalmist, "serve the Lord with gladness," (Psalm 100:2); and why? "Know ye that the Lord he is God, he hath made us," (Psalm 100:3).

Secondly, when we had by Adam's fall *unmade* (as I may say) ourselves in that which was the best in our making, the image of God, and had by losing that, lost and undone ourselves, will we serve him that recovered and saved us from that lost condition? Zacharias will tell us in his song, "We were delivered out of the hands of our enemies, that we might serve him," (Luke 1:74), *servati ut servi.*

Thirdly, will we serve such a Master that admits of all to be his servants, that tender their service, and, "casts out none that come," (John 6:37), and chooses his servants, not by the nobleness of their birth, or the greatness of their abilities? "Not many wise men after the flesh, nor many mighty, not many Noble are called," (1 Corinthians 1:26); poverty, impotency, lack of parts may make us unfit for the service of man. But God, as Elihu in Job, "accepteth not the persons of Princes, nor regardeth the rich more than the poor," (Job 34:19), when farms, oxen and wives kept those invited guests from the marriage supper (Matthew 22:2), the King (for so he is called) sent forth his servants, "into the Lanes and Streets of the City, into the highways and hedges to bring in the poor, and the maimed...and the blind," (Luke 14:18-21, 23). Children may be too young to do service to man, yet, "Suffer the little children to come unto to me," (Mark 10:14) Christ says; and how did he accept and justify the children's, "Crying Hosanna to the Son of David?" (Matthew 21:15,16).

And for service itself, will we make choice of that which is first most honorable? And great persons will admit of none that may eclipse their greatness; is there any service in the world so honorable, as the service of God, to be servants unto the King of Kings? The greatest peers of the land have thought themselves honored much by being servants to a King, and have accounted their places of office their greatest titles of honor; some Princes have more gloried that they were the servants of Christ, than if Monarchs of the world.

And which adds to the honor of this service, are not our fellow servants (however the world despises them) all honorable? "Those excellent ones, the Saints in the earth," (Psalm 26:3), and glorious angels in heaven; so one of them said to John, "I am thy fellow servant," (Revelation 19:20).

Yet more, what is it that we serve for? Is it not expressed by that which is most honorable on earth? "A crown, and that incorruptible, a Kingdom, and such as cannot be moved," (1 Corinthians 9:25); and which much increases this honor, it is that which the poorest Saint is capable of, and the Apostle would have special notice taken of it, "Hearken my beloved brethren, hath not God chosen the poor of this world rich in faith, and heirs of the kingdom?" (Hebrews 12:29).

Secondly, do we not desire that service which is most gainful? And matter of gain is much looked at in every service, "In all labor" said the Wiseman, "there is profit," (Proverbs 14:23); and we shall find it the wicked's pretence in Job for not serving God, "what is the Almighty that we should serve him, and what profit should we have if we pray unto him?" (Job 21:15). So see what the Prophet says, "It is in vain to serve God, what profit is it that we have kept his ordinances?" (Malachi 3:14).

Servants will not usually hire themselves, without Covenanting or hope of wages, "A hireling looks for the reward of his work," (Job 7:2); and those services that bring or promise most profit are most sought after. I desire no more, then that we would in truth hold ourselves to this, make choice of that service, which will be most for our profit, and then I am sure the Lord shall have our service, and ourselves that profit, which all the services in the world will not afford.

1. In all others, though some pay comes to the servant, yet the chief gain is to the Master; in God's service it is otherwise. So Eliphaz, "can a man be profitable to God, as he that is wise may be profitable to himself, or is it gain to him that thou makest thy way perfect?" (Job 22:2,3). All our labor in God's service is *for our own profit*; God has the glory, we the benefit, "it is for our good," (Deuteronomy 10:12, 13).

Secondly, the least service done to God (if in truth) shall not go without its recompense; hear the Lord making this good, "Who is there even among you, that would shut the doors for nought? Neither do ye kindle a fire under my Altar for nought," (Malachi 1:10); in the world such as are constant workmen to any man, will not think much to do some small chores (as we call them) without looking for any pay; not so in God's service. Was it not said to him that had improved the one pound committed to him, "Well done thou good servant, because thou hast been faithful in a very little, have thou authority over ten cities," (Luke 19:17)? What acceptance found, "the poor widow's two mites," (Luke 21:3)? And what reward promised to, "a cup of cold water given to one of these little ones in the name of a Disciple?" (Matthew 10:42).

Thirdly, do we desire that service which has all the comforts and encouragements that may be desired or found in any service? For many services may promise much gain, yet they are soured with such present slavery and hardship, as better ones lose hopes of profit, then undergo the bitterness and toil of the service; so it is not in the service of God.

Would we first have this encouragement, to be sure of help, and such as may enable us to do the work required, which we cannot do by our own strength? Know then that there is no work which God requires of his, but he helps them to do the work required; to instance only in that of Prayer;

does God command, "Call upon me in the day of trouble?" (Psalm 50:15)? We are in trouble of conscience, dejection of spirit, it may be in some spiritual desertion, or other distress, and would willingly pray, but truly can say with the Apostle, "we do not know how to pray as we ought," (Romans 8:26); hear an encouragement, "The spirit helpeth our infirmities." Who would not serve such a master, that will never put his servants on any work, to which he will not put his helping hand? The Church acknowledges this of God, "Thou Lord hast wrought all our works in us," (Isaiah 26:12), says the text, "for us," the margin says in our Geneva bible.

Secondly, would we have this encouragement, that though in many things we offend all, and must say with the Apostle, "The good that I would, I do not, and the evil that I would not, that I do," (Romans 7:29). We would yet hope that our unwilling filings shall be forgiven? Hear the Lord by the Prophets, "I will spare him as a man spareth his own son that serveth him," (Malachi 3:17); that of the Psalmist I conceive looks this way, "Rejoice the soul of thy servant, for thou Lord art good and ready to forgive;" that in which your servants weakness causes him to fail, your goodness moves you readily to forgive.

Thirdly, would we in times of danger have hopes of comfort and protection? And nothing more exposes to the malice of men and the devil's service than the service of God;

hear the Lord by the Prophet, first threatening, "therefore will I number you to the sword, and ye shall bow down to the slaughter, because when I called ye did not answer; when I spake ye did not hear, but did evil before mine eyes, and did choose that in which I delighted not: therefore thus saith the Lord God, behold my servants shall eat, but ye shall be hungry; my servants shall drink, but ye shall be thirsty; behold my servants shall rejoice, but ye shall be ashamed; behold my servants shall sing for joy of heart, but ye shall cry for sorrow of heart, and shall howl for vexation of spirit," (Isaiah 65:12-14). The confidence and comfortable experience of those three worthies in Daniel are comfortable instances, "Our God we serve is able to deliver us, and he will deliver us," (Daniel 3:17, 28); Darius said to Daniel, "Thy God whom thou servest continually, he will deliver thee," (Daniel 6:16, 20).

Fourthly, would we be in such a service, in which though some hardship in the entrance or progress, yet the end will be comfortable? (and children will take a bitter pill, when they may have sugar after it) then know that the hardest and most uncomfortable part of God's service will undoubtedly end in comfort; for however, "no chastening for the present seemeth joyous, but grievous," (Hebrews 12:11); yet, says the same Apostle, and that on a serious computation, "I reckon that the sufferings of this present time are not worthy to be compared with the glory which shall be revealed," (Romans

8:18); and he gives the reason, "for our light affliction which is but for a moment, worketh for us a far more exceeding and eternal weight of glory, whilst we look *etc*," (2 Corinthians 4:17, 18).

If the Lord has blessed these considerations and encouragements to work our hearts to this service, and we desire so to, "serve God, that we may please him," (Hebrews 12:28, as the Geneva Bible reads it) and have interest in those privileges of his servants; take we notice of the conditions required in our service, "it must be, 1. In truth; 2. With all our heart." It is in truth without hypocrisy, with all our heart, without partiality. God looks that his servants should be truly his, and wholly his, and he requires both the inward man, and the whole man.

What it is to serve God in truth, will appear by that wherewith it is joined, and that in this very duty, "Fear the Lord, and serve him in sincerity and truth," (Joshua 24:14); so twice in one Chapter, "To deal truly and sincerely," (Judges 9:16, 19), and things are then said to be true, in which there is no deceit; so Christ said of Nathanael, "behold an Israelite indeed," (John 1:47), the Greek is ἀληθῶς *truly* an Israelite, "in whom is no guile:" God is then served of us, "in truth", when in all services the hidden man of the heart goes along with the outward man.

It was the testimony that Solomon gave of David, "he walked before God in truth," (1 Kings 3:6). Hezekiah said, "remember me O Lord, how I have walked before thee in truth," (2 Kings 20:3).

That all our services to God must be done, "in truth", will *appear in the following:*

1. Because that God whom we serve, is a, "God of truth," (Deuteronomy 2:4; Isaiah 65:16). The Psalmist says, "of God, thou desirest truth in the inward parts," (Psalm 51:6).

Secondly that Christ, in and through whom all our services are accepted, "is also truth," (John 14:6).

Thirdly the Spirit, which is the chief helper in our services, is, "the spirit of truth," (John 1:14, 17; 15:26; 16:13).

Fourthly the Word, which ought to be the rule of our service, is, "the word of truth," (2 Corinthians 6:7; 2 Timothy 2:15; James 1:18). So that we may truly apply that of Christ, "The hour cometh and now is, when the true worshipers shall worship the Father in Spirit and truth; for the Father seeketh such to worship him," (John 4:23, 24).

For inquiry what is to be done, that all our services may be performed, "in truth:" for this two things are required.

First, that we do all by a right rule, which is only that Word, which (as we have heard) is the word of truth, or as the angel called it, "the Scripture of Truth," (Daniel 10:21); hear Moses, "Ye shall observe to do as the Lord your God commanded you, you shall not turn aside to the right hand or to the left," (Deuteronomy 5:12, 32), that is, as Masius on Joshua 1:7 observes out of Rabbi Levi, that Moses explains himself, "Which thing so ever I command you, observe to do it, you shall not add thereunto, nor diminish from it. In vain (Christ says) do they worship me, teaching for doctrines the commandments of men," (Matthew 15:9); therefore the Apostle exhorting, "to give up our bodies as a living sacrifice, holy, and acceptable to God, which is our reasonable service;" adds, "prove what is the good and acceptable will of God," (Romans 12:1, 2).

Secondly, our service must be done to a right end; what that is, the Apostle has told us, "Whatsoever ye do, do all to the glory of God," (1 Corinthians 10:31). Truth in every service *eyes God*; hypocrisy may look as a squint at God, but directly at *self ends*, and seldom or never looks at God in any service, but through spectacles of self-love: such a zealot was Jehu, serving God, so far as he might serve his own ends; therefore what he brags of as, "his zeal," (2 Kings 10:16), God threatens to avenge as murder (Hosea 1:4, 10, 11). Such was Ephraim, "a Heifer that loveth to tread out the corn," not caring to plow, because that was only labor, o present self-advantage, and therefore she will work in that, in which her own turn might be served, by feeding on the corn she trod out, according to that in the Law, "Thou shalt not muzzle the ox, when he treadeth out the corn," (Deuteronomy 25:4).

Such were those, "teachers, that caused Divisions and Dissensions" in the Church, "and by good words and fair speeches deceive the hearts of the simple, which serve not our Lord Jesus Christ, but their own belly," (Romans 16:17, 18): that is, says Aquinas, do not in their preaching aim at the glory of Christ, but their own gain.[3]

Would then Parliament men, Magistrates, and Ministers have assurance that they serve God (in their several stations) in truth? Let them ask their hearts, what rule they have acted by, what their ends, have they been and are to serve God, to advance his cause and glory in their places, or by their places to serve themselves? It is known what Christ once said, "Whosoever will come after me, let him deny himself," (Mark 8:34); and certainly we shall never with Caleb, "follow God fully," (Numbers 14:24), while *self* stands in the way. The kingdom in Church and State has suffered much by disaffected Malignants; and means have been and are used to discover them, and I wish they were all found out that are the troublers of our Israel; yet give me leave to suggest, that there are yet too grand Malignants, whom we are either not willing to take due notice of, or too inclinable to favour, under which

---

[3] Aquinas *in loc.*

the complaint is that the kingdom does yet suffer, in that they have too much influence on committees and votes; I mean self and alter ego, our own interests, and favour of friends.

But that I may not forget myself, and how far the time is already spent, I proceed to the second condition required in our service of God; It must be, "with all the heart:" by heart, we are not to understand that fleshy part in our natural bodies, but the spiritual part, our souls, often joined and required in this duty of serving God; the latter (as I conceive) explaining the former, in that of Moses, "What doth the Lord require of thee, but to serve the Lord thy God with all thy heart, and with all thy soul?" (Deuteronomy 10:12, 13). So in the following chapter; that is, with all the faculties of the soul, the understanding the eye of the soul, the Memory the souls recorder, the affections, the seat of the soul, with all the rest.

And this God *requires:*

First, because the soul of man, whose chief residence, and (as I may say) chair of state is in the heart, though enclosed in the body as a prison, yet it is there, as Joseph in the Kings prison in Egypt, Kings it were in that prison, having as a Sovereign the command of the whole man, "The heart of a wise man (Solomon says) guideth his mouth," (Proverbs 16:23). Which way the heart sways, that way goes the tongue, the Messenger and Interpreter of the heart; when God's cause has the heart, it shall have the vote. I could give you other places, where the eye, the ear, the feet, are disposed and commanded by the heart; so Eliphaz of the whole man, "Why doth thine heart carry thee away?" (Job 15:12). Here observe, that the Apostle calls the *heart*, the *man* in that expression, "the hidden man of the heart," (1 Peter 3:4), because it disposes of the whole man, *mens cujusque is est quisque*, every man is as his mind is. God, therefore in his service, requires the heart; for that brought on, like the master wheel in a clock, will turn and bring on all in man.

Until God has the heart, no hope of real goodness is found in any other part, "There is not a true word in their mouth, within they are very corruption," (Psalm 5:9) or as others read, "their heart is vain," a vain heart has a lying tongue:, "again their heart imagineth destruction, and their lips speak mischief," (Proverbs 24:2); where malice is within, and mischief without. So you find another Psalm, "ye imagine mischief in your hearts, your hands execute cruelty," (Psalm 58:2); mischievous thoughts have bloody designs, what evil the heart contrives, the hand is ready to act; therefore David prays, "incline not my heart to any evil thing, to practice wicked works with men that work iniquity," (Psalm 141:4), implying, that he should not refrain evil actions in life, unless his heart restrained from evil inclinations.

What show or beginning of goodness seems to be in any, that does not come from the heart, like, "Hosea's morning cloud and early dew," (Hosea 6:4), go away and not continue, what caused the word like the seed sown in those three sorts of ground come to nothing? It was because it was not, "received into a good and honest heart," (Luke 8:15); what occasioned that unsettledness and revolt? "They were not steadfast in his covenant, their heart was not right with God," (Psalm 78:37). It is the Apostles caveat, "take heed, lest there be in any of you an evil heart to depart from the living God," (Hebrews 3:12); an evil heart may seem to hold with God for a time, it cannot hold long; if the ground is not good, such hearts are apt to decay. Hypocrisy mostly ends in apostasy.

I shall touch on the other branch of this condition requiring not only the heart in God's service, but *all* the heart, which takes in both the entireness and cheerfulness of the heart.

For first, God cannot endure, "a divided heart, that halting between two opinions," (Hosea 10:2), or as the margin makes note for us, two thoughts, "between God and Baal," (1 Kings 18:2); like the River Hebrus and Thracia, that runs so slowly, as hardly discerned which way it runs; a staggering man is easily thrown down; those, "feet which are halting are apt to be turned out of the way," (Hebrews 12:13); when *your* Thames (your fast running river) in its slow time comes to a standing halt, later the ebb of the river presently follows. Indifference in religion is the next step to apostatizing from Religion.

Nor secondly, will God accept or delight in that service which is, "done grudgingly," (2 Corinthians 7:9), and as it, "were of necessity," (1 Peter 5:2); when we are kept in God's service, as unruly beasts in a Pasture, "by a hedge of thorns," (Hosea 2:6), the Lord's own expression, some inconvenience would come to ourselves; it may be loss to our estates. If we should desert the service; but let the hedge be trodden down, or some gap made in it, the beasts breakout; let the cause we formerly adhered to, be in some disrespect, or not advancing our private designs, or a way open to avoid the inconvenience that hedged us in, some it may be, whose march before was in the same cause, as Jehu's (2 Kings 9:20); their pace as Asahel's, "light of foot as a wild roe," (2 Samuel 2:18), now like the, "Chariot wheels of the Egyptians, they drive heavily," (Exodus 14:25); are as lame as Mephibosheth (2 kings 19:26), or like the bed-rid palsy man, did not come until brought on by others (Mark 2:3), or as the unwilling guests, not, "come in, until in like manner compelled," (Luke 14:23).

Take two or three short uses of both these branches; First, does God in every service require the heart? Then know, that no service shall find acceptance with God, unless God in that service does find the heart, "no melody to the Lord in singing Psalms," (Ephesians 5:19), unless, "we sing with grace in our hearts," (Colossians 3:16); God is not satisfied that his word has the ear, when the heart is gone after the world (Ezekiel 33:30, 32): *that* prayer will not reach heaven, nor find access to the throne of Grace, unless with Hannah, "there be a speaking in the heart," (1 Samuel 1:13). Such people are by Christ rejected as hypocrites, "that draw near to God with their mouths, when yet their hearts are far from him," (Matthew 15:8).

Learn the true cause why the outward man is so unwilling to yield to God, the feet as hardly brought to tread in his courts, the ears so dull in hearing, the tongue so silent in speaking for God and his cause, the eye so dim in seeing the wondrous things in God's Law; the heart the fountain of life and spring of motion is not yet quickened and moved; hear Moses making this good of the eye and ear, "The Lord hath not given you a heart to perceive, and eyes to see, and ears to hear," (Deuteronomy 29:4); a dark understanding has a dim eye, and a deaf ear; the Apostle gives this as the reason of the Jews blindness and stubbornness in receiving Christ, "That even unto this day, when Moses is read, the veil is upon their heart," (2 Corinthians 3:15).

Would we then give God the service of the whole man? Do we do that which Solomon advises, "My son give me thine heart," (Proverbs 23:26); that being in truth given to

God, will unloose the tongue, "My heart is indicting a good matter, my tongue is the pen of a ready writer,"(Psalm 45:1); will open the ear, "Lydia's opened heart," (Acts 16:14) worked an attentive ear; will speed the feet, "I will run the way of thy Commandments, when thou shalt enlarge my heart," (Psalm 119: 32; Psalm 86:12).

Nor will the heart only bring the whole man to God, but will also hold him close to God; when David had prayed, "Teach me thy way O Lord," promised obedience, "I will walk in thy truth", he adds as a special means to keep him to this, "Unite my heart to fear thy name," (Psalm 86:11); no part will willingly fall off from God, while the heart remains knit to God; no bands or strings tie so fast and sure, as those of the heart.

I have done with the duty and conditions required; I desire to borrow more both of your patience and time, for pressing the reason used by Samuel to enforce the duty, "for consider what great things he has done for you."

The word translated consider, is in the Hebrew, וְאָו Videte.[4] See, applied so well to the eye of the mind, as of the body; and implies, that all God's works of mercy, should be so carefully and continually remembered of us, as those things are, which we have still in our eye.

---

[4] See Buxtorf.

That the serious consideration of God's mercies, ought to enforce the service of him, take that of Moses, who having enlarged the greatness of God's both pardoning and supplying mercies, he shows what God expects from them, "And now Israel, what doth the Lord thy God require of thee, but to serve the Lord thy God with all thy heart, and with all thy soul?" (Deuteronomy 10:12). So Joshua, after a brief rehearsal of all those great things which God had done for them, infers, "Now therefore serve the Lord in sincerity and truth," (Joshua 24:14); the Apostle presses the same, "I beseech you by the mercies of God, that you give up your bodies a living sacrifice, holy, acceptable unto God, which is your reasonable service," (Romans 12:1). So again, "Wherefore we receiving a kingdom that cannot be moved, let us have grace, whereby we may serve God acceptably with reverence and godly fear," (Hebrews 12:28).

The reason the text may reach us personally is found in considering these four particulars points. 1. What great things have been done for us? 2. That all these great things have been done by the Lord 3. That these great things should not be forgotten, but still in our eye. 4. What great things, that have been done for us, should work in us? I shall do little more than name the three first, then expound the last.

That great things have been done for us, in our counsels, in our wars, by land, by sea, many fine designs blasted, dangerous plots discovered, great expectations frustrated, great armies defeated, great victories obtained; great assistance from our brethren of Scotland, great faithfulness and courage in commanders and soldiers; great supplies from the renowned and well deserving city of London, and others well affected, "even to and beyond their power," (2 Corinthians 8:3); great mercies in keeping the devouring sword from our habitations in these parts, sheathing the sword of the Pestilence; hopes of preventing the, "evil arrow of famine," (Ezekiel 5:16); preserving the union between the two Nations; who can do less than with admiration acknowledge these great things done for us.

Secondly, that all those aforementioned great things are at the Lord's disposing, and whatsoever done in them was done by the Lord's hand, I might clear by particular texts, if either the time would give leave, or the things questionable; I shall only touch upon the Lord's managing of the war, (a special means by which these great things are done) will it not appear, that the Lord of Hosts by his own arm got our Victories, if we consider first the time when the Lord began to do these great things; and *that:*

First, in relation to ourselves. Was it not when Bristow lost, that our Armies scattered in the North and West? Did not the Lord begin to, "remember us, when we were in a low estate," (Psalm 136:23), and the spirits of many so low as their condition?

Secondly, in relation to our enemies, was it not when their hope and confidence was at the highest? As several of the Kings letter's witness a little before Naseby fight. The time in which these great things done, were not most of them done within the compass of a year, and that without the loss of much blood? *Incruente victoriae*; when the Lord began to work, did he not work a *quick work* in our Land? Dianna's Temple at Ephesus, took above 300 years to build, and the Temple at Jerusalem took 46 years (John 2:20); but to make a world in *six* days, must be a work alone of an Almighty God.

Or, if we consider the instruments, whom the Lord used for working these great things; was not that noble General looked on by the enemy, as David by Goliath, with contempt and disdain? (1 Samuel 17:32). And the army itself, as those 300 select men of Gideon's army were, it may be by those that were diminished, "and sent every man to his own place"? (Judges 7:3, 6, 16).

That these great things which the Lord has done should not be forgotten, all the *monuments* of God's great works recorded in Scripture may be lessons for us; the first visible great work that ever God did, the Creation of the world, appointed to be remembered one day in seven, by annexing it as a special reason for the observation of that day.

The Psalmist minding us of God's great works would have us know, that, "the Lord has made all his wonderful works to be remembered," (Psalm 111:2, 4); and in the former Psalm called on us to do it, "Remember his marvelous works, that he hath done," (Psalm 105:5). And I do not doubt but as heretofore you were minded by one of your remembrancers[5], care is taken, that they may, "be written for the generations to come," (Psalm 102:18); and that not only in our own, but in that language, as it may be said (if possible) in all the Kingdoms of the earth, as in a following Psalm, "The Lord hath done great things for them," (Psalm 126:2).

But what should those great things which God has done for us work in us? First to give all the glory to God, "Not unto us O Lord, not unto us, but unto thy Name give glory," (Psalm 115:1). Justinian is said to have made a Law, that no master workman should put up his name within the body of that building, which he made out of another man's cost; our own Histories tell us, that when Wickham, then Chaplain to Edward the Third, was by him made overseer of the work for repair of Windsor Castle, that those three words which he caused to be inscribed upon the great Tower, *hoc fecit Wickham*, this *made* Wickham, had not he construed them another way, had lost him the King's favour; hear the Psalmist trebling this

---

[5] Mr. S.M.

charge upon those whose greatness makes them too apt to take too much unto themselves, "give unto the Lord O ye mighty, give unto the Lord glory and strength, give unto the Lord the glory due to his Name," (Psalm 29:1, 2). Implying that great persons in the things of God should carry themselves like themselves, go through with what they undertake; when they begin to give to God, never give *over giving*, until they have given to God all that is his due.

But what glory does God expect from great ones, not alone that of their lips, to give God a few good words, to speak well of his name; but chiefly that of their lives. Their authority will be less prevailing for suppressing those evils, to where their bad examples give encouragement. Naturalists report of the bird *Ibis*, of which many in Egypt, especially in the City of Alexandria, that it eats up all the garbage of the city, but leaves *something* behind it, that is more noisome then any filth it had eaten.[6] Another writes, that it will devour every serpent it meets with; but from the egg of this bird comes the most hurtful of all Serpents, the Basilisk, the sight of which kills;[7] I forbear to apply, but not to pry, that in all those who are God's on earth, may be found always joined, that which the Psalmist says of God in Heaven, "Thou art good and doest good," (Psalm 119:68).

---

[6] Gesnerus.
[7] Pierius.

Secondly, has God done great things for us? Then certainly he expects great things from us, "Unto whom much is given, of him shall be much required," (Luke 12:48); do not let those to whom God has given great opportunities, and furnished with answerable abilities to do great things for God and his cause, put off God with a little. We have not been served with half victories, half successes, such would not have served our turn, and be sure he will not be served with half services, half or partial Reformation. God will not be dealt with, as the unjust Steward did with his masters Creditors, where, "and hundred was due, to set down fifty," (Luke 16:6); or with, "Ephraim's cake not turned," (Hosea 7:8). As the words are expounded, half baked, baked on the one side, raw on the other; a mixture of truth and errors. It was a great failing in Hezekiah, "That he rendered not to the Lord according to the benefit done unto him," (2 Chronicles 32:25). And rather should we mind this, if we consider that though the Lord (blessed be his name) has done great things for us, yet he has not done all that we expect, and of which the Church and State stand in need. Many ships have come near the haven, has by storms been driven into the main, and there perished. Some have been cast away near the shore, as that in the Acts (Acts 27:39, 40). If we expected no more, then what is already done, we might make the bolder with God: but there being much yet for the Lord to do, settling the Church government in the Kingdom, the suppression of errors, the turning of the King's heart, the rescue of Ireland, and (which is hoped, will not in due time be forgotten) the recovery of the Palatinate; it will be our wisdom not to fail God, lest hereafter he fails us: and turns that hand which has here been for us, against us; think we of that in the Prophet, "In all their afflictions he was afflicted, and the Angel of his presence saved them, in his love and in his pity he redeemed them, and he bare them and carried them all the days of old; but they rebelled and vexed his holy Spirit, therefore he was turned to be their enemy, and fought against them," (Isaiah 63:9, 10).

I presume we are satisfied in this, that it is better to have all the Nations of the earth our enemies, then God to be our enemy; often speeches there have been of forces from other parts, and Malignants in all parts hope (if they dare speak out) for a day; but if our ill requital of God, and the sins yet amongst us, make God our enemy: we need fear no power or combination of all enemies in the world; that war alone is truly to be feared, in which God fights against a people.

The Egyptians never spoke of fleeing, until they found God against them, "let us flee say they from the face of Israel: for God fighteth for them against the Egyptians," (Exodus 14:25). The Philistines feared not to fight with Israel, until they conceived God appeared for them:, "The Philistines were afraid and said, God is come into the Camp, woe unto us;" and again, "woe unto us, who shall deliver us out of the hand of these mighty Gods?" (1 Samuel 4:7, 8).

Thirdly, has God done great things for us? We appear, according to our place and power for God, in the same kind in which he has appeared for us, first he has brought in, and united the hearts and hands of the best affected in the kingdom; let him in anything concerning his glory have our cordial help an furtherance.

God has subdued the necks of our enemies to us and we should not be unwilling to submit ours to his yoke, to come under his government; we may read the doom of those that said, "we will not have this man to reign over us; Those mine enemies, which would not that I should reign over them, bring hither and slay them before me," (Luke 19:27). And we should take heed; Christ has a, "rod of iron" to break them to pieces, that will not come under his Scepter (Psalm 2:9).

For you (Honored Worthies) the Lord has put power into your hands to reform and settle the government of the Church; and we find (and bless God for you) that is your endeavour and resolution for this work, which was the vain confidence of that people, "the bricks are fallen down: but we will build with hewn stones; the Sycamore trees are cut down: but we will change them into Cedars," (Isaiah 9:10).

For the doctrine of the Church, as we trust by God's direction and blessing, the ground-work of which will be so firmly laid, as none of, "those foxes" mentioned by the Church, shall be able to earth in it, "to spoil the tender grapes of this vine," (Song of Songs 2:15). So we do not doubt, but the hedge about it by your civil sanction will be made so strong, as no, "wild Boar out of the wood shall waste: nor wild beast of the field devour it," (Psalm 80:13); neither heresy, carnal policy, or violence shall prevail to corrupt or suppress it.

Fourthly, the Lord by blessing your counsels and forces (we hope) has given you two kingdoms already; will we trust in his good time, give you another: let your study be to make these three Kingdoms the Kingdom of Christ; then doubt not but he will preserve his own; and no more probable way, then by providing, that, "the Gospel of the Kingdom," (Matthew 9:35), or elsewhere, "the Word of the Kingdom," (Matthew 13:19) may be powerfully and sincerely preached in all parts thereof; and to this end, that all possible ways may by your wisdom and zeal be thought on, for rising a fitting encouragement by competent maintenance for many poor parishes.

It has been often charged on Henry VIII, for his disposing of the lands belonging to Monasteries, that he did not out of them first take care for the erecting and endowment of Free-schools, and provision for poor church livings in all the parts of his dominions.

Give me leave to speak freely, after ages cannot expect the like opportunity to that, which God has now put into your hands, by those means which were formerly given to the Church, to raise some encouraging comfortable provision; and if you should give all, you shall but do that to God and his service, which David once in a case looking this way, said, "of thine own have we given thee," (1 Chronicles 9:14).

Since the Popes of Rome have changed *Petre pasce* into *Petre rege*, the Church has had many Rectors, few Pastors; yet we acknowledge it our duty, it is expected from us, and we desire to do it according to those abilities the Lord has given, to feed the flock committed to our charge; but we hope it will not be thought reasonable that such as desire plentifully to feed others with spiritual food, should either decline such poor places, or live on a little better then starving allowance.

I have thought it a great aggravation of the Egyptians' unkind dealing with the posterity of Joseph, in requiring their full tally of bricks, and not allowing them straw for the making of them; when as their forefathers were furnished by Joseph with corn to save their lives (Exodus 5:7-8).

Fifthly, has God done great things for us, and that when we were able to do little for ourselves; did, "He remember us in our low estate?" (Psalm 136:23). Let us not forget God, when those things in which he is so much concerned, are in a low condition; does not Christ, the blessed Spirit suffer much in their Deity, and does not God suffer much in his Law, in the Scriptures, in his ordinances, and ministers?

So, I beseech you the name of God be dear to us, and everything in which the honor of God is any way impaired; let all blasphemies against God, against the Scriptures be suppressed; the Jews were so careful of the former, that if one saw never so small a piece of paper under his feet, in which was any writing he was to take it up, and take heed of treading upon it, lest in that paper there might be found written the name of God; and for the Scripture, they were so tender of its esteem, that if any occasion in his journey to have with him the book of the Law, he might not carry it on the back of his beast, but in his bosom next to his heart.[8]

Of those two great persecutions against the woman and her child, raised by the Dragon and Serpent, "that flood of waters cast out of the Serpent's mouth," (Revelation 12:4, 25) most endangered them; the first under the heathenish persecuting Roman Emperors, caused the Church only to flee and hide herself for a time; the latter, which were the several heresies then sprung up and spread in the Church, in danger to drown her.[9]

---

[8] *Schichardu de jure region Hebreorum.*
[9] Mr. Obadiah Sedgwick.

But I am in this (though formerly in my meditations) happily prevented by a more learned tongue in this place; yet give me leave to those heresies which break out at the first rising of this flood, to add one which was before the first of those recited, and the rather because by hell and the serpent again vomited, it had its rise in Arabia, and condemned under the name of the Arabian heresy, affirming that the souls of men did die and consume with the bodies, and that at the last day they should again rise with the body, Origen in a Synod confuted it.[10]

And surely if ever God's truth and church were likely to be carried away and *over born*, it is now, with this flood out of the serpent's mouth, belching forth such fearful blasphemies, as former ages scarcely heard of; what one way to stop this flood, the Apostle has told us, "There are many unruly and vain talkers and deceivers, whose mouths must be stopped, who subvert whole houses, teaching things which they ought not for filthy lucre's sake," (Titus 1: 10-11).

Another way, which the Lord has stirred up the Honorable Houses of Parliament to use, is the setting apart a solemn day of humiliation for this Judgement and the sins that brought it; in which I hope there will flow in such a tide of tears, as shall by God's blessing overmaster this flood and

---

[10] Osiander cent. .3.c.1. Anno. 251.

drive it back into the serpent's mouth, from where it came, as your own tides do the fresh rivers at their flow.

Or that there will be such heat and fervency in the prayers of that day, as like the fire that fell on Elijah's burnt sacrifice, it shall lick and dry up the water of this flood, as that did the water in the trench (1 Kings 18 38); the fervent prayer of one single man did once dry up the spring head of such a flood as had almost overflowed the whole world; I mean that of the Arian heresy.

When Arius[11] and his heresy came to Constantinople, the chief City of the Empire, and was by his followers to be brought in great triumph to the chief Church, Alexander the Bishop of Constantinople, the day before humbly and earnestly sought God, that he would either take Arius out of the world, before he entered into that Church, or else that he himself might not live to see it; the event or effect of his prayer what it was, I believe you have often heard, that Arius going on the day designed with great pomp towards the Church, was taken with some pain in his belly, went aside to ease nature, and voided his bowels.

Or that all these heresies expressed by, "smoke out of the bottomless pit," (Revelation 9:2), shall like smoke the higher they grow, be the nearer their scattering, or like floods when at the height, their ebb is at hand. However we do not, if

---

[11] Osiander cent. 4. 1 2. c. 38.

our sins and neglect of means do not hinder, but that the God of truth, who sits on the floods, will in his good time, "Say to this deep be dry, and to this flood, hitherto shalt thou come and no further, and here shall thy proud waves stay," (Isaiah 44:27, Job 38:11); and make good that of the Apostle, he speaks of the heretics of those times, "They shall proceed no further, for their madness [so the Geneva; and the Greek ἄνοια will bear it] shall be made manifest unto all men," (2 Timothy 3:9).

Sixthly, has God appeared in his wisdom, goodness and power in doing great things for us? Do not let our power and parts be lacking, in doing what we can for God. The Lacedaemonians made the statue of Apollo, their god of wisdom with four ears, and four hands, to show that wisdom should be much in hearing what she ought to do; and much in acting, what she knew was to be done; and the rather let us use what we have from God, for God.

First, because we have all from him a promise, one day to be made like him; and in the meantime votes and speeches are not more truly registered in journal books, than they are in God's.[12] God sees the hearts, what the designs of everyone are; as not long since out of this place, "all things are naked and opened unto the eyes of him with whom we have to do," (Hebrews 4:13); what account then will they give to him, that

---

[12] Mr. M.N.

either have done nothing for God; or it may be what they can do to hinder and retard his works?

Secondly, there is no such way to make what God has given us, useful to ourselves, as by using it for God and his cause whatsoever is against God, his Glory and Truth in restraining and repressing according to our power and place. When the Philistines thought to have surprised Sampson suddenly, the best weapon that he found was, "a new jawbone of an ass, wherewith he slew a thousand men," (Judges 15:14, 15); after the victory and his praising God for it, "he was sore athirst, and called on the Lord, and said thou hast given this great deliverance into the hand of thy servant, and now shall I die for thirst?" (Judges 15:18) See how the Lord dealt with him in this extremity, "God clave a hollow place that was in the jaw, and there came water there out; and when he had drunk, his spirit came again, and he revived," (Judges 15:19); God used that for supply of his personal needs, which he had used for God against the enemies of God.

Seventhly, has God done great things for us? Let us take heed, that we do not undo those great things, and hazard the undoing of the three Kingdoms, by doing great things against them, and ourselves; we may by our divisions undo all in a few months, which the Lord has been doing for us in some years, when we were of one heart, and went about the work as one man; and the enemies greatest hope is by dividing to weaken and subdue us.

It is said, that there is a stone in the island Sycrus, that floats above the water being whole: but broken in pieces sinks to the bottom.[13] In that conflict between those six brethren who are called by the Historian *ter gemini fratres,*[14] the *Horatij* and the *Curiatij,* had the three wounded *Curiatij* not divided themselves, but held together against that one surviving of the *Horatij,* they would have not lost the day, their lives, their Country's liberty.

And to prevent this division, give leave to mind us all, of two last branches of the two first articles of the Covenant, concerning our endeavours for uniformity in Religion; the widest breeches in affection too often rising from differences in profession; the war between the Turk and Persian both Mohammedans, raised and fomented from their differing practice about their worship.

And as it is well observed, the Prophets amongst God's people did not prophesy of destruction, until the Kingdom came to be divided: a King of Israel, and King of Judah; so it is worthy taking notice, what brought from God the division in the Kingdom; you shall find that, "Solomon marrying strange wives," (1 Kings 11:1), he gave leave to all of them, to have the

---

[13] Piu. l.36.c.7.
[14] Lev. D. 1. l.1.

service of their several gods, "wherefore the Lord said unto Solomon, for as much as this is done by thee: I will surely rend the Kingdom from thee; and I will give it to thy servant," (1 Kings 11:7, 8, 11). Solomon suffering divisions in religion, punished with division the Kingdom in his sons' days; Solomon tolerated the worship of false gods; and Rehoboam found ten tribes revolting; and proving false to him (1 Kings 12:20).

Eighthly, we consider what great things God has done for us. Then I presume it will not be thought unreasonable, that those be considered whom the Lord has used as instruments working these great things for us, the Commanders, Officers, and Soldiers. I hope the complaints are not so true as some reports them, that many which have jeopardized their lives in this service, for lack of pay, are hardly able to support the lives of themselves and families. When the Chronicle was read what Mordecai the Jew had done for prevention of the treason against Ahasuerus, he asked, "what honor and dignity hath been done to Mordecai for this," (Esther 6:3); It cannot (blessed be God) be said, as his servants said to him, "there is nothing done for him", I hope our annals that shall record what great things the Lord has done for us, shall not be without some lasting monument of what has been done, as for those Commanders and Soldiers, by whose valour and faithfulness the Lord has wrought these, so especially for the poor and maimed; I shall leave this, with only an honorable mention of that pious and charitable work of that virtuous Prince Edward the 6th, who upon Bishop Ridley's Sermon exhorting to charity, set apart and endowed three great houses in London than at his disposing for three several sorts of poor people.

Ninethly, has God done great things for you? And that in a short time! Then I trust Honored Worthies Petitioners shall not wait long to receive a little from you; it may be read what Job wished to himself, "If he withheld the poor from their desire, or caused the eyes of the Widow to fail, then let mine arm fall from my shoulder blade, and mine arm be broken from the bone; for destruction from God was a terror to me, and by reason of his highness I could not endure," (Job 31:16, 22, 23).

The Parliaments of England are looked upon and resorted unto as that, "Pool of Bethsaida in Jerusalem, that had virtue to make whole all that stepped into it, of whatsoever disease they had," (John 5:2, 4); I hope none shall have cause to complain, as that poor impotent man to Christ; I have had an infirmity of many years continuance, yet it is curable, if I could get into this Pool; and I am come to it for cure, have waited long; yet here is my misery, Sir, "I have no man when the water is troubled to put me into the Pool, but when I am coming, another steppeth in before me," (John 5:5,7).

It will be an honor, and is the earnest prayer of all the best affected; that we may say of this Parliament, as they in the Prophet:, "The Lord bless thee o habitation of Justice and mountain of holiness," (Jeremiah 31:23); that in all Committees and proceedings may be found that in another Prophet, "Let judgement run down as waters, and righteousness as mighty streams," (Amos 5:24); Let justice as waters have its ordinary course, run its proper Channel, no stoppage by delays or Privilege in reference to just debts; and let it be of such power, that like a mighty stream it may bear down on all oppositions of friends and greatness whatsoever; if it is a righteous cause, let it carry against how great or how many so ever stand against it.

"I consider saith the Preacher, all the oppressions that are done under the sun, and behold the tears of such as were oppressed, and they had no comforter" Ecclesiastes 4:1); the word translated *tears*, is well observed to be in the Hebrew, *Lachryma*,[15] a Tear; it may be either to show that there should be so much compassion towards the afflicted, as one single tear or the first tear that they shed should win relief, or as one observes to show the neglect of pity in those that have suffered the oppressed to wait and weep so long to crave help, yet still delayed, as they could weep no more, had only but one tear left, and it came from here, because the oppressed had no

---

[15] דְּמָעַת

comforter to relieve them, the oppressors had friends to support them, and keep off hearings and execution of justice.

But however it may be thought, that the tears which fall from the oppressed fall to the ground, yet let causers of these know, that their tears ascend so high as heaven, are there turned into flashes of lightning and thunderbolts, and will come down in vengeance. The Lord by Moses assures it, "Ye shall not afflict any widow or fatherless child; if you afflict them in any wise [*either by not doing justice or delaying it*] and they cry at all unto me, I will surely hear their cry; and my wrath shall wax hot, and I will kill you with the sword, and your wives shall be widows, and your children fatherless," (Exodus22:22-24).

Observe how dangerous it is not to hear the cry of the afflicted; Elihu says that hereby, "they cause the cry of the poor to come unto God, and he heareth the cry of the afflicted," (Job 34:28); and their cry will bring down wrath, even that of the sword; and surely we may justly fear, that the partial swaying the sword of Justice in this kingdom, was not the least of those sins that provoked the Lord to draw out his sword of vengeance; and further, that not hearing the cry of the afflicted, may not only find a deaf war in God in times of distress, "Whoso stoppeth his ears at the cry of the poor, he also shall cry himself and not be heard," (Proverbs 21:13); but also may keep off mercy from theirs. It is one of the arguments that the Preacher uses to stir up unto works of charity and liberality, "Give a portion to seven, and also to eight, for thou knowest not what evil shall be upon the earth;" none knowing how God may hereafter deal with them or theirs, whither, "his sons come to honor, or be brought low", and that it may be just with God, that their widows and fatherless children may find as little succour and compassion from those that seek to, as they formerly showed to widows and the fatherless.

It is a received rule, he that does not hinder or restrain sin or injury, when it is in his power, makes them his own; and as it is said in reference to alms, a poor man is ready to starve, if you are able to relieve, and do not do it; he dies, you are his death's man, "*si non pavisti, occidisti;*"[16] so he is wronged by some great person; they that have power in their hands to right him, and do not do it, the wrong done becomes theirs, and they shall answer before God's tribunal for wronging him.

And for the poorer sort that may flee to this Parliament for shelter, let me commend that practice of Job, "I delivered the poor that cried, and the fatherless and him that had none to help him; the blessing of him that was ready to perish came upon me, and I caused the widows heart to sing for joy," (Job 29:12, 13). It may be some are fled to this high and Honorable Court, that in their estate and hopes are ready to perish through long and chargeable attendance; there is a blessing to

---

[16] Ambrose.

be had in relieving these perishing ones; oh that there might be a godly strife, who should step in, and by appearing for them to get this blessing.

It is Solomon's advice, "open thy mouth for the dumb," (Proverbs 31:9), such as either cannot, or may not speak for themselves; and again, "open thy mouth, judge righteously, and plead the cause of the poor and needy." It is an honorable memory, that James, the 5th King of Scots, has left behind him (as King James his grandchild relates in his *Basilicon doron*) that he was called the poor man's King. It will not be the least honor to this Parliament, if among others of those great things done by it, renowned it may be to posterity for being the poor man's Parliament, to right and relieve those that have no other means to right and relieve themselves, but by fleeing to this shelter.

It has been a great honor to be the King's attorney, solicitor, or sergeant; is it not far greater to be these to Christ? Who will one day say, "Inasmuch as ye have done it to one of these little ones, ye have done it to me," (Matthew 25:40).

Great persons are in Scripture expressed by the *Sun*, which affords his influence so well to the lowest shrub, as the tallest cedar, shines as comfortably on the poorest cottage, as much as the stateliest place. And I could with that as great ones take some content in having their pictures resembling them (as they say) to the life, so in this they would resemble their pictures, which if drawn as they should, would eye and look towards the poorest and meanest person that looks upon them; Radolpus Habspurgius, seeing some of his guard put by some poor persons that were coming towards him, was much displeased, charging them to suffer the poorest to have access to him, saying that he was called to the empire not to be shut up in a chest, as reserved for some few, but to be where all might have free access to him.[17]

Ninthly, has God done great things for us? Let the serious consideration of this work in our souls be a sad and deep humiliation as for our other sins, so for doing so little for God, that we have not improved our places, abilities, and opportunities for God and his cause as we ought and might have done; and who because of this may not justly lay his hand on his heart, and with Pharaoh's butler say, "I do remember my faults this day," (Genesis 41:9).

And surely we had not more cause to have former days of humiliation to crave of God the doing of great things for us, than we have now to be humbled that we have done so little for God. Hear the Lord by the Prophet, "I will remember my covenant with thee, and I will establish unto thee an everlasting covenant; then thou shalt remember thy ways and be ashamed," (Ezekiel 16:61); but what were those ways, will

---

[17] Schichardus.

be found in the former verse, "thou hast despised the oath, in breaking the covenant," (Ezekiel 16:60); I kept my covenant with you, therefore be ashamed when you remember how you have broken covenant with me. It has been enjoined that the covenant should be read at the end of the last sermon upon our days of humiliation, and pity it should be omitted, that if nothing in the sermons, yet our breech of covenant might humble us, and send us away with bleeding hearts.

Tenthly, in the last place, has God done great things for us? Being truly humbled for former failings, and resolved to do in our places according to our utmost power, what these great things call for at our hands, let us be encouraged to go on without fainting in God's and the kingdom's cause, with all constancy and cheerfulness, notwithstanding all mountains of oppositions, and difficulties that may seem to obstruct the way; the due consideration of all the former passages of God's providence and appearance, may much strengthen our faith in and dependence on him for the time to come.

I have sometimes thought, what might be the reason, why the Psalmist in two Psalms grounds his assurance of God's help for his Church, on the Lord's making heaven and earth, "Our help is in the name of the Lord, which hath made heaven and earth," (Psalm 122:2 and Psalm 124:8); why did not the Church build their confidence rather on particular experiences, as on that God which brought us out of Egypt, opened a passage for us through the Red Sea, so miraculously led and fed us in the wilderness; drove out the Nations before us in Canaan, by grasshoppers subdued giants, *etc.* I conceive it was to support the Church against those three usual grounds of distrust; either the work to be done is great far beyond our power; or secondly, our wisdom fails, we can see no probable means to expect it; or thirdly, it may require so long a time, as we may say with Balaam, "also who shall live when God doth this?" (Numbers 24:23)

The relying on that God who made heaven and earth, will help against these.

First, is the work great? Consider, was there ever so great and glorious a visible work done, as the making of this great and never sufficiently admired frame and fabric of heaven and earth, with all creatures in both? Which yet the Lord made by a word speaking; he spoke the Word and they were made.

Secondly, are we brought to such straights and extremities, the wisdom and counsel even of the ablest are at a stand; and no human probable way to bring our desires and designs to pass? Consider, was there ever any more unlikely means to produce such a world of wonders in the variety and excellency of the creatures: then out of that confused chaos? Can that Almighty Creator, which made all things of nothing, lack means to bring to pass in heaven and earth whatsoever he pleases?

Thirdly, are there so many great things to be done, as we may not only say with Ezra, "neither is this a work of a day or two," (Ezra 10:13), but rather with Joel, in another case, a work that may hold, "to the years of many generations," (Joel 2:2), if the same spirit of perverseness should be found in succeeding ages; as in the present, of which we may too truly complain, as the Lord by the Prophet, "we would have healed Babylon, but she is not healed," (Jeremiah 51:9); and yet which is worse, and makes the wound in a manner at present incurable, "it refuseth to be healed?" (Jeremiah 15:18).

Yet consider, however, the Lord is slow to wrath, and may be long in destroying; as that sinful Jericho devoted to destruction, not destroyed in less than seven days compassing; but for works of mercy, the Lord made a complete world in six days; when, "the time to favour and build up Zion is now," (Psalm 102:13), that shall be made good in the Prophet, "a little one shall become a thousand, and a small one a strong Nation, I the Lord will hasten it in his time," (Isaiah 60:22).

I could turn you to several places, where the Prophets Isaiah and Jeremiah raise arguments of confidence in God from the Creation, as Isaiah 44:24-26, 45:17-18. I will instance only in that of Jeremiah, "Ah Lord God, thou hast made the heaven and the earth by thy great power and stretched out arm, and there is nothing too hard for thee," (Jeremiah 32:17). Will we then rest on God for finishing every work of mercy, which he has begun, and that from the consideration of what great things he has already done, let me for our better encouragement close up all with that of Christ to Nathanael, "Because I said unto thee, I saw thee under the fig tree, believest thou? Thou shalt see far greater things than these," (John 1:50). That we may have this faith and trust in God, and find this grace and mercy from God, we ought always to return with our prayers and praises to the Lord.

*FINIS.*

# THE FALL OF ADAM

[ORIGINAL TITLE PAGE]

## THE
## FIRST MAN
OR,
A Short Discourse
OF
ADAMS STATE
*VIZ.*

1. Of his being made a living Soul.
2. Of the manner of his Fall.

BY JOHN GREENE

---

*LONDON*
Printed for *Benjamin Allen* in Popes-head-Alley,
*Anno Dom.*
1643.

# ADAM A LIVING SOUL

"And the LORD God formed man of the dust of the ground, and breathed into his nostrils the breath of life; and man became a living soul," (Genesis 2:7).

*What is living soul?*

A living soul is a man in innocency. The Scripture says, "the first man was made a living soul." Adam was perfect in reason, knowing all natural things in the fullness of their nature, worth and excellency, observing and taking pleasure in the glory of God, which shone in through and over all the works of the most high, so that there was not any beauty or virtue in anything, but he had the sense and sum of it within his own capacity or reason. He gave names to creatures suitable to their natures, strength and vivacity. Moreover, he knew the beauty of things in their several causes, how they were knit together, and how this union made a goodly harmony; and although there were many things in nature contrary to each other: yet as they were ordered by the wisdom of the wisest, did unanimously agree with, and help each other. All things then were good both in themselves and in their several effects. He did not know weakness or death in anything, until death first fell on him, and then issued forth from him in and on all other creatures by his fall. He knew himself to be the chiefest of the way of God, and that God had more respect to him than to any of all his creatures (I speak comparatively) so that there was nothing that could gain on him or rob him of his heart that was outside of him. Put all things together outside of him and all will scarcely prove equal to him, either for beauty, wisdom or heavenly knowledge. He knew God to be the upper ground of all things, both in their beings and motions; and if there was any excellency in any of the creatures (as in all there was some) it was the scatterings of the same breath which breathed first life in him. As the light and beams of the Sun are guides to conduct our eyes to the seat and throne of the Sun, where it is in its being beauty and full form, the glory of God to convey Adam to the throne of the high, full and beautiful majesty; in whom he knew all things concentered.

Doubtless, he knew all things were born up by the same arm which first gave them their beings, and he which gave them their beings, (I mean the creatures) must be greater in being then all; neither could they flourish any longer, then by the fullness and efficacy of that mighty being, they were replenished suitable to the greatness and glory of the things which are seen, must be things which do not appear. And if the heathens (as Paul says) knew God in his invisible eternal power and Godhead, surely Adam in these things knew much more. God made man upright (the Scripture says), I conceive the meaning of that word may be *either*:

First, this with his heart fixed and placed only on God; which way so ever he turned himself, or on whatsoever he looked; all that he took pleasure to see was, at first, God in all man's mind upward to holiness, but now downward.

Or secondly, the word is a Metaphor, taken from a line or rule by which men measure or square out any particular work, which rule they ought not to exceed. So man had then his bounds and limits beyond which he ought not to have passed, and in his compass might have walked with pleasure.

Or thirdly, it is set in opposition to crookedness. Man in *innocency* did not go awry (yet) but passed straight forward in the most pleasant paths, neither turning to the right, or the left hand. But now he leaves the straight line, and walks in ways contrary to truth, righteousness and peace, often times striving how he may be most crooked and most forward, reeling to and fro like one who is drunk. The Scripture makes mention of a living soul, and a quickening spirit. Adam is the one, and Christ is the other. I shall endeavour according to my light (or knowledge), to show the meaning of both. First *for a living soul.*

The first and lowest meaning I conceive is this, to be a living soul, is to be truly a man. Other creatures, when they were formed, were said to have life in them, but none besides man, were said to be a living soul.

Secondly, a living soul is a man indeed, with a lively and active principal of reason, by virtue of which he was able to distinguish of things according to their worth and excellency and also filled with wisdom, by which he saw how all causes by their several influences and operations came to be most excellently united, and that the first cause which gave life and breath to all the rest, was not only *primum mobile*, but also *summum bonum*, so that as his reason served him to couple all things together, so it also raised him to see how all things were coupled, and that he who did thus unite all, and overshadow all, by the influence and power of his eternal being, was more glorious and greater than all, which considered, caused him there to rest, and in that to take full content.

Thirdly, a living soul signifies (as it has reference to that estate in which he was in this way *upright*) immutability and duration, and He (meaning God) breathed in him the breath of life. This breathing or breath of God, was the great power and glory of God, molding him into that glorious estate, and preserving of him in that estate, until he left it, or rather it left him, of which I shall speak more afterwards.

There was not the least tincture of death, that came on man while he remained in this estate of innocence; neither in his body or mind; mortality was the consequence of sin, "If thou eatest," says the Scripture, "in dying thou shalt die." While he obeyed he was fresh, fair, and flourishing, without any defect, as all things else were. O! How goodly a thing was man until he turned from *Adam*, life, to death. Yes, life was the flower of his being, declaring him glorious, until death entered in, and diminished the powers of life.

But because it lies in my way; I will speak but briefly of this second thing leaving it to its due place, I mean, *Christ is a quickening spirit.*

There are three things also to be considered for its opening. First, a quickening spirit is such a one, who must have the fullness and substance of all shadows and outward appearance *in him*. *Spirit* signifies the *perfection* and *beauty* of anything. The other word put to it makes it in this way *much*, namely, this perfection and beauty in its altitude and vivacity is the highest, for nothing can be higher, more ample, or more lovely in being, then things truly spiritual, or the *Spirit*, the cause of spiritual things. Life is in Christ, because the power of the infinite and eternal being dwells completely in him. One of the highest names which Christ himself sets forth God by, is this, that he is a Spirit, and Christ is this God spiritually understood.

Secondly, a quickening spirit is one who has not only this in himself, but he has power to *convey* this spiritual beauty on whomsoever he will. The *Son* quickens whom he will says the Scripture, he can (by the mighty operation of his life and spirit) transform all into the Image of the same glory if he will. Although Adam had life in him, (such a life as I have spoken of) yet he did not have any power to convey the least dram of this life to any; which manifests that this life was much lower and weaker than that life which was in Christ.

Thirdly, the third meaning is this, that he is appointed and set apart of God for this end: the Scripture says, he was made a quickening spirit, as Christ is God, so it is no robbery for him to be equal with God: and so he is neither under command, neither in that consideration does he stand in need of any courtesy or dignity from the God-head, but as he is God in our nature, clothed with human flesh, so he is set apart by the authority of the eternal Father to several offices. He does this by virtue of conveying grace, knowledge and all divine privileges and spiritual blessings on the sons of men, because there is no power in us of ourselves to bring life and divine strength to us. Therefore, God has appointed an infallible means near himself which is able to conduce to the uttermost of that end; the happiness of a poor dead soul laden with sin and guilt, that Christ is designed by the Father to quicken and raise him and in all things it is his care to manifest himself faithful.

# THE MANNER OR WAY OF THE FALL OF ADAM

It is a great question, *How Adam fell?* That he is fallen is no question, but the manner and way of his Fall is that which is very disputed, and seems to be a great mystery. Everyone concludes he was upright for a reason, and as long as he in this way continued, death and mortality did not enter on him.

The thing first to be considered is, whether he had this breath of life or uprightness (of which I have already spoken) of, in, and by himself, or by any other means. There is none that will say this of himself; for he neither had his being, neither his well-being of himself. For the Scripture says, "God formed him of the dust," and, "God breathed in him the breath of life." If this is from God, the *question* is, whether he had it absolutely, or by way of dependence. By absolute, I mean, whether he had it so inherently established in him, as that by the keeping or losing of it (I mean in that consideration) he had no relation to God. If you will say he had it in this way established in himself, then what is become of that maxim, both of heathen writers, or of religious writers, and of the Scriptures, that say, "We live, move, and have our being *in God?*" Surely if God without a helper made all things of nothing, then by the same power that all things were made, they must be every moment upheld and preserved, or else all things once again would turn into nothing. And if all things, then Adam and the things of Adam (for he was one of the things that was made), or further, if God, or else God had given this power to Adam wholly from himself, either there were at once, "two Gods," and so consequently no God, or else God had ungodded himself to make Adam, "a God," which is high blasphemy to think. If I know anything of God, this is one thing that I know, that although God is most excellent and full of goodness, so that his goodness is communicated and spread abroad, in, and over all things, yet he does not absolutely part from any piece of his glory and goodness, so as that he does leave its managing alone to any creature. The beams and heat of the Sun refreshes and strengthens many creatures, and yet take away the Sun from its beams, and the beams will lose both their virtue and being, and creatures will lose their comfort. So there is much of the sweetness, goodness and glory of God in many creatures, as so many beams issuing forth from the glory of God; but take away God from the creatures, they will lose their sweetness, their glory, and their very being also. It is a general tenet held by the major part of men, yes and good men also, whom I love and honor here in England. That Adam had a power, in, and of himself to stand in that estate in which he was created: (I should be sorry if by mistake I should wrong any, and I am confident that I have heard some reason for it.) If he had power (I mean *of himself*) to stand, how did it come to pass that he fell? Is there any desire of evil in good, or misery in happiness? His standing was good, and doubtless so was the power by which he stood, whether it was in himself or otherwise; reason will tell us, (and as I have said Adam had the height of reason) so long as man keeps his reason, which brings him to felicity, he cannot press after misery. It is said he had power to stand or fall; I conceive that so long as he stood he had a power by which he stood; when he fell, it was because he lacked this power. If he had kept the power, or rather, *the power had kept him*, he would have never fallen; he could not have power to fall (I mean in that estate which we call *innocence*) for falling from a good estate to a bad is through a defect of power. If Adam fell from life to death, from felicity to misery, it was not because he had a power to fall but because this power did not uphold him. It is true, while he stood he stood, and he stood by a power, and had not that power failed him, he would have stood longer: but suppose it is objected, that the power by which he was assaulted was greater than that which in that estate he was possessed with, and so by means he disobeyed; for, says the man, "The woman which thou gavest me, gave me of the tree, and I did eat." To which I shall in this way first answer, if we consider him before he was fallen, or before the very act of his fall, the power which was against him, was not equal to that which he had. For if Adam knew God, and served God, (his desires and inclinations being only to it, accounting this his greatest good, knowing him to be most excellent and his will to be most delighted in all this arising from principle of knowledge and perfection which he had) then how can he be greater than truth, when truth is strong, yes *strongest of all.* The Devil comes to him with this lie in his mouth, "If thou doest disobey thou shalt live and be as God," and with such like words. Adam, considered in that estate, might in this way have answered the Devil (and his principles would have led him to it) I know what God has said is true, he is God, and cannot deny himself, he has laid his command upon me, and given me bounds beyond which I may not go; if you say otherwise, you have lost your knowledge of God, in whom all goodness and blessedness consists, and are become a Liar. It is that the Devil is said to be great and to have power, and so is sin also, but it is in reference to our weak estate, when we compare him and his power with things which are not, to be; and the things which are, to lose their beings, but he being a deceiver is still deceived. Until Adam was deceived, he never thought as the Devil did, and had his power remained with him he would have never had been deceived; for as long as he stood, it was the power that kept him. I confess if Adam's estate was partly good and partly evil, then (if we may use such and expression) he had power to fall. But if it was wholly good, as the Scripture says, that God saw all things which he had made, "and it was good;" and doubtless men was one of the greatest of these good things, if not the greatest of all. Then in that condition he might not have any inclination to evil, but his inclination to evil was his fall; so that we see Adam's estate was wholly good, and in every good thing so long as it is good, it is by a power kept in its goodness. If Adam had the breath of life breathed in him, then so long as that breath of life remained in its glory, death could not enter upon him.

But I shall secondly answer in this way. If we consider Adam either after his fall, or in his fall, (that is to say, as he did fully) the power against him was greater than that which was with him, otherwise he would not have fallen. If Adam was envenomed with evil (as he was), the Devil was the envenomer, and the cause is greater than the effects, although many times the effect does exceedingly open, and give light to the nature of the cause. The Devil is a fountain of lies and deceits, and by his subtlety in lying, filled Adam with deceit. It is much to be thought, that in all the Devil's words which he used to deceive both Adam and Eve, we heard not of a word of reply to gainsay his discourse. Indeed, Eve tells him of the obligation and band that God had laid upon them, but when he charges God with falsehood, and hatred, and the like we read not of any reply to clear God, made by them, but rather a full entertaining of his discourse; by which I conceive, that no sooner were there motions suggested to them by the Tempter but forthwith were they entertained by them; yes, and happily without any debate, whether they were right or wrong, good or evil; had they retained their knowledge and strength while they were under the temptation, they would have then easily freed themselves from the efficacy of the temptation; but it seems to me, while they were *being* tempted, or when, they *were* tempted, the power departed from them, and so the temptation had efficacy upon them, otherwise they would have resisted the temptation. Often times the act of evil, and the act of good, is performed with equal delight, although the consequence prove various. So happily while they were in the act of sin, they did not know it, but afterwards the guilt and the shame which followed caused them to know. If ever the Devil did show himself like an Angel of light in any of his wiles, as often he does, surely one of the fairest dresses he put on, was when he tempted Adam, "Ye shall be as gods," says the Tempter. It was not altogether so gross as to tell him he should be in God's stead although he lacked but a step to it, for to be equal, is to divide, and to divide is to destroy; for to seek to have two God's at once is to seek to have none at all. Perhaps the Devil took the same method with Adam to bring him to misery, as he himself practiced when he first wrought his own misery.

But to hover no longer, we see Adam has lost his integrity, and the man in that case is undone; how shall we find out the way of his loss? This I shall endeavour to do by discoursing upon two things; the first is, how or from where Adam had the power to stand? The second is, how he lost it? For the first of these I shall speak more brief, because I have spoken of it already. All power is from the highest power, which is from God, from where Adam had his; yet not so as that God parted from it out of his own hand, for then it would have lost its power, and have been no power at all. Divide the streams from the fountains, and they will quickly lose their natures and their names too; the power which with-held him was a momentary supply from God, which while he stood firm, kept him as firm as he was when first he had his being. He at the first was formed after the image of God, every minute that image was preserved and kept in him by the same power which fashioned it in him. The image of a thing is the representation of the thing, although it is not the thing itself. Adam was formed after the image of God, this image was a description or draught of the glory of God upon him, although (I confess) not so glorious as that draught which is drawn forth on Christ. So far is the glory of Christ beyond the glory of Adam. For what says the Scripture? "The first man is of the earth, earthly; the second is the Lord from heaven." This image of God in Adam was the truth or spirit of his life, and life cannot be maintained lively without some spring: the fountain or spring which maintains all true beings, is God, so that we may (I suppose) conclude that God gave him his life, and the same God did keep it, so long as it was kept.

The second question is, *how Adam lost his integrity?* And here (I confess) I should be sorry to speak anything contrary to reason or religion; yet if I should miscarry, I should be glad to be informed. And above all things, when I am speaking of the things of God, I am most afraid of dishonoring or charging him with folly. For, "let God be true and every man a liar." But now I have begun to speak, I shall freely deliver my thoughts. So why do I think he lost it? As I have said, it was God that upheld him while he stood, so it was the same God that did withdraw or kept back the power and so Adam fell. Had he kept the power or rather the power kept him, he would not have fallen; but God was pleased, for the magnifying of his name, to withdraw himself from him, and so left him under the power of the temptation, by which he was overcome. It was the power, or God, that made him strong, and had this continued with him, he could not have been weak. The Devil might have assaulted him long enough with all the power and subtlety he could get together, and all his batteries would have been in vain, if he had the same strength by which he was preserved, and it still remained with him. So now here we see Adam almost in a moment high and low, rich and poor, strong and weak, happy and miserable, his glory and sense is gone, and left in the hands of cruel enemies, and these exercising tyranny upon him and triumphing over him. But there are some *objections* which rise up against what I have said. One is to this effect, "Whether in so saying we make God the Author of sin?" For so the objection says, "If God withdraws or withholds himself from Adam, and the Devil comes up against him (he being now weak) is necessitated to yield, and to sin."

To this I answer, that in a positive and strict sense he is not, for as all things he is most clear and free from sin in himself, and in his own nature, there being no uncleanness or unclean thing that can enter into his Tabernacle. So he is as free and clear concerning the acting or working any evil, either in or by himself. For how can any unclean thing come forth of the thing that is clean. Sin is not in him, therefore he cannot act or commit sin. The Devil is positively evil, sin dwells inherently in him, and is engrafted into his being. It was his action and motion which had an influence upon Adam, by virtue of which he was drawn into the same condemnation with himself, and did actually as well as the Devil commit sin. Concerning the temptation or working of sin in Adam, God is altogether clear, and to be discharged and the Devil and Adam himself to be blamed. If God gave Adam a Law, and this Law was good as all things else were then, and the goodness of the Law was either in its own nature, or because God gave it, God being the highest good cannot diminish or destroy the least good which he would have done, had he broken his own Law. It is one thing to take away a power which is in itself good, or to take away a power by which any good thing is preserved, and it being taken away, of necessity the good thing must perish. And it is another thing to commit sin, and manifestly to act it, when the power which kept the good thing, and the good thing itself, which was kept by the power, are both departed. To be an author of anything, is to be a worker or actor of the thing, or else (which is higher) to give being to the thing. God is the author of all good or goodness, either as all good or goodness is concentred in him, or as all good is wrought and brought to light by him, therefore God cannot be the Author of sin, I mean in a full and strict sense, because sin does not have its being in him, he did not beget it, neither does he cherish it in his bosom. Sin is a deprivation or lessening of good, therefore it cannot be in God, because he is not only good, but good in the highest degree, says the Scripture, "Sin is of the Devil, and if of and from the Devil, then not of and from God." So that we see the Devil may sin, and Adam may sin, and yet God is not to be the author of sin.

But in the second place, I answer in this way, that in an accidental way God may be said to occasion sin, for had it been the good pleasure of God to give Adam the same power always, by which at first he stood in his integrity, he would not have sinned. When the light is gone darkness will cover the face of the earth, and the light's departure is occasionally the cause of darkness, so is the departure of God from Adam, occasionally the cause of his fall. Our Saviour says, he came not to bring peace, but a sword, and yet the Angels said, at his coming into the World, on earth peace, good will towards men; the truth is, our Saviour came to bring peace in a plain and strict sense, and that was the end of his coming, and yet occasionally came a sword. There are many things done in the World which are sinful, which actions God has a special hand in, and yet God is clear from the evil of those actions. Suppose one man kills another with a sword, here is God first permitting such an action, otherwise it could not be done, for if he pleased he could hinder it.

And secondly, here is God giving power to the man, whereby his action is done. If he puts forth his hand, if he strikes the stroke, it is by a power, if you will say it is by the power of nature, I will answer, that it is the God of nature that gives nature its power.

No, thirdly, here is God accomplishing some end in this business, here is either some Judgment shown upon the person, or some example given for caution to the world; and yet God is free from the envy, mischief, and evil of the action. Surely if God can free himself from evil in actions of this nature, (in which so much of him is to be seen) we may easily acquit him, when he does but withhold that power, by which we are kept from sinning or evil actions. Many things that may occasion sin, may be wholly free from sin itself, unless it is in the occasion or accident (had I a better expression for the present in my thoughts, then the word occasion, I would speak it). Suppose a beautiful woman passes by in the streets, perhaps her heart is wholly and heavenly, or otherwise she is very intent about the business in which she is employed; some man looks on her, and lusts after her. She does not think in the least degree of this business, and does not even know the man sinned in lusting after her (speaking in terms of human knowledge); I hope every man who knows this will free this woman from the evil of this action, and never commit the sin of lust again. So God may occasion evil and yet be free, yes far from the evil itself, the rain does not fall for a long space on the earth, in the meantime the earth parches and becomes dry, and the grass withers. I hope none will say that the rain parched the ground, or withered the grass. To conclude this first *Objection*, if God will withdraw, Adam must sin, and yet Adam is the sinner and God clear from his sin.

The second *Objection* (of which I shall speak more briefly) is; whether God is not the original cause of sin?

To this I answer no, unless I am mistaken in the word *original*. To be the original cause of anything is (I conceive) to be the first cause in giving the thing its being and denomination, and such a cause as that the thing which is the effect must partake of the nature of the cause, we often times are speaking of the bewailing of our original sin, we mean that sin which Adam had originally or as the fountain in him, he being the stock from whence so many withered leaves and branches of impiety do appear in us. It was in him, it spreads forth on all mankind from him. The fountain is the origin of the streams; why, because the streams were first in the fountain. God does not give sin a being, and yet without God sin could not be. Happily to some it may appear strange, yet in my thoughts it does appear true; I mean, so, God does not give sin a being as he gave life to Adam, he breathed life in Adam, and then he lived. God does not breathe, or work sin in any, his breathings are pure and undefiled. All things to which he positively gives being from his own workings are good, and I mean thus, when I say without God sin could not be, either that it is his pleasure that sin should have a being, otherwise he could have prevented it. Or else that he suffers it; or else that he makes way for its being, which in a sense, yes and in a true sense he does, for sin would not have been among men, if Adam had stood firm. Adam could not stand when the power by which he stood was taken from him, and so he fell; and it was God who kept back the power by which he stood. If reason or Religion, or both would teach me to make God a lesser cause of sin, were it for his honor, I should gladly do it, for above all things I desire to honor God; God is originally good and originally the cause of good and therefore cannot be originally the cause of evil. Evil and good are at the greatest longitude from one another. While Adam did well God was near to him, but when he sinned he thrust God from him by his sinning.

The third *Objection* is *this*:

How God will be cleared to be righteous and just in his dealing towards Adam, in the withdrawing of himself, when there was no other means for him to be kept in his integrity?

To this I *answer*:

That God can do no unjust thing, whatsoever he does is righteous, as he himself is righteous; all his works are by and from himself. The Potter has power to make and design his vessels for honor or dishonor, at his pleasure, because they are his workmanship. If the Potter is to make these vessels by the commandment and power of some other; he is to do according to his commission. But if he does it without command and is left to his will, who is then to contradict him, in what shape so ever he makes these vessels or to what use whatsoever he puts them? So if God is under any higher command than himself, and had from that power a command to make Adam in that form which he did, and to keep him continually in that form and state in which he was made, then if he withdrew the power which kept Adam in this estate (as he did) he would have done unrighteously, and must have been accountable to him from whom he had the command. But God is above all Law, there is none above him to compel him to do anything, or to give him a Law, to which he might owe subjection; neither is there any equal to him, by which he might be entreated, therefore he is a Law *to himself*. He measures out all his ways and actions by the line and rule of the god-head. As there is none but himself to compel himself to action, so neither does he ask advice of any but himself for the performance of the same. What he wills is a Law, and if he wills anything, the thing he wills is according to knowledge, wisdom and judgement, and he sees and judges all things according to the excellency of his own nature and being, which is according to truth, yea according to the highest truth. It is a maxim general and true, that God is the highest being, and perfection itself, that he is without addition or diminution, if so, let him do what he will, he cannot err or do unrighteously. If he is one huge piece of spiritual glory, and all things in him are infinite, as he himself is, in beauty, praise and perfection, how is it possible to think he can do any uncomely thing; if he had pleased he might have made Adam in another form, either higher or lower at his pleasure, and who should have contradicted him. If he will make his creatures glorious, and suffer them to be blasted immediately, so that he may bring in a greater glory to make himself more glorious, who shall control him, this is the weakness of man, that because we by our low and weak judgement and reason cannot find out the high God in the way of his righteousness: therefore will we seek to make him unrighteous, when we should rather (like Paul) who speaking of the great way of God in shutting up all men under unbelief, cry out that his Judgements are unsearchable, and his ways past finding out. All unrighteousness arises from some defect and unevenness in men's ways, if God's way was not complete, no if this work in the leaving of Adam to himself, was not glorious and admirable; or if we can tell of any that will come after him, and rectify or amend his work, then he will confess his fault, and to him owe the tribute of praise. Is it possible, to be thought, that he which knows all things at once, which shall be throughout eternity and by the same wisdom and knowledge orders the being, the form of the being, the time of the being of everything which shall be, should do anything contrary to himself, and if he does nothing contrary to himself, he cannot do anything unrighteously, because as I have said, he is a Law to himself? It is a true rule, that where there is no Law, there is no transgression, then if there is none to be a Lawgiver to God, and his knowledge and will are the rule by which he measures out all things; who then can say what he does in done amiss, although he does whatsoever he will.

But secondly, I answer in this way, that God was not anyway engaged to keep Adam in that estate in which he was first created. Had he been engaged to keep him, he must have kept him. If God had made Adam any promise, that as he had created him righteous, so he would still keep him in his righteousness, God must then have regarded his promise, otherwise he would have been unrighteous; Adam could challenge nothing at his hands, because he promised nothing to him. There are two things that do principally bind, either a Law or a Promise; there was neither of these upon God, to tie him to preserve Adam in that estate in which he first created him. Doubtless Adam in that had been happy, had God said thus to him, "As I have made thee righteous, and beautified thee with mine image, so I will forever keep thee." The reason is this, God cannot change or deny himself, he is faithful if he says anything, he knows he must effect the thing which he has spoken, therefore he is wise and careful in all his sayings. When God speaks anything, he speaks it *of himself*, therefore he must necessarily speak the truth, and he is careful to perform what he speaks; as he is to speak it, otherwise he would not deal truly. One great difference between the estate of Adam and the estate of one in Christ Jesus, is this, that to such which are in Christ Jesus he has engaged himself by *Covenant and Promise*, that he will also keep them in Christ. And this is clear, that he never failed in the performing of his promise; but he did not so to Adam. Indeed he gave him a Law, and bid him keep it, but he did not tell him he would help him to keep it. The case is much alike between the condition of Adam and such who are under the Law, and look for happiness by it; men might have been happy that were under the Law, could they have kept it, but the Law could not give of itself life, neither could those that were subject to it keep it. So Adam could not keep that Law to which he was subject, neither was there life or power in that Law to keep him. What is to be said? God might very well blame, yes, and punish Adam for the breech of his Law, because he was his Creator, and was above him; yes, and under that consideration he sought God as his very being; but Adam did not have this to charge God, but must lay his hand on his mouth and be silent. By this we may see that God does not only manifest himself to be righteous in the withdrawing himself from Adam, but even by it his righteousness shines abundantly.

The next *Objection* is this, that God commanded impossibilities. For in this way the *Objection* is stated, if God gave Adam such a Law, which he knew he did not have power to keep, how then could he look for obedience to that Law, which was impossible for him to obey?

I answer affirmatively, that God may if he please, command things impossible for men to do, God is the Sovereign Lord, and as it is his royal prerogative to make and give Laws, so by the same prerogative may he make what Laws he will. He may bid me to do what he pleases and lay a penalty on me if I do not do the thing that pleases him, yes, and execute the penalty also, and yet remain just and righteous. The reason is, because he is Sovereign or chief, there is none to sit in Counsel with him when he makes or ordains Laws, or to control him by saying, let them be thus or thus. And if he wills a Law impossible for man to keep yet this is a good Law, he is our Creator, he gave us our beings, and the form of our beings, had he pleased, he might have given us other kinds of beings, and who could or dares control him, and so might he (if he pleased) dissolve our beings, and yet be as free from control, and shall we allow him the greater and not the lesser. If God gave us our beings which were good, and gave us a law, in the keeping of which we might have kept ourselves in this goodness, and yet we had not power to keep this Law. Did he not do well? Doubtless he did (or if he did not, then let us blame him). The Laws which God gave to Moses, seems to me to be as hard to keep, as that which he gave to Adam in Paradise, for none have kept it. And you in your catechism it says, *Is any man able to keep the Commandments?* The answer is *no*. And yet none either does or dares blame the law, or the Lawgiver. Surely if men do, and may command things which are impossible, God may.

There are many Laws for the well-being of a Kingdom or State (these being grounded on the word of God) which Kings and Governors make, and yet how few of these are there duly observed, any by reason of our weak and infirm estate, it is impossible fully to keep them, and yet who blames either the Laws or the Lawmakers. Some have run (at least in my apprehension) into a strange absurdity, by denying this point, which I am now speaking of, which they have done by placing a power in man to do God's will or command of himself, and in effect saying, that it is in the will of man to believe, to repent, and consequently to be a self-Saviour. But to the matter in hand, our Saviour tells the Jews, that to work the work of God is *to believe*, and John tells us, that the Commandment is *faith* or *believing*. It appears that faith is a commandment, and yet it is impossible for flesh and blood to believe, for the Scripture says, "It is a gift from God; so that we may see." God did not only command things impossible for Adam to do or perform, but also for all his posterity, and yet he remains faithful and just because he does not change his Law even though men fall. There are many things which God does, which in our eyes would seem unrighteous, no, inhumane and cruel, and yet he is just in so doing. God bids Abraham to sacrifice his Son, and it is plain, if he had so done, he must have murdered his Son, and we know that in the Commandment, God says, "Thou shalt do no murder." And yet we may not say, that God did any unjust thing in commanding or bidding of Abraham to observe such a command. If God then does give a law, and yet does bid men to do things contrary to that Law (and yet does no evil) why should it then seem a harsh thing to us if God gives us such a Law which we cannot fulfill or obey.

Here are two things to be considered about this business of Abraham, and I hope I shall not swerve from my discourse.

The first is, whether Abraham had sinned if he had obeyed God in the sacrificing of his Son Isaac or no? I conceive all without scruple will answer negatively.

The second thing is, whether God did any evil in commanding anything for Abraham to do contrary to a former command?

I answer that God may repeal or call back any of his laws, if he pleases; or else if he pleases to bid anyone to do anything contrary to any of his commands. The reason is this, because by all the positive Laws or Commands of God, we are tied and engaged, and not God. If God bids us to do a thing, we are to do it. If by and by he bids us to undo that thing, or do something contrary to it, we are *still* to do it. A master may bid a servant to do a thing, and after bid him to undo it again; and yet the servant is to obey his Master. So it is the Sovereign or *Prerogative Royal*, for God to command what he will, and it is our duty to be obedient to that which he commands.

Where God promises us anything, then he is *engaged*, but not when he commands. When the Israelites were to depart out of Egypt, God (not purposing that they should return again) bids them to borrow jewels and raiment of the Egyptians, and the Israelites never restored the things they borrowed from the Egyptians. And I also suppose that when God bids the Israelites in this way to borrow it was not his intent that they should pay them again. And I bring these instances only to possess the reader, that God by his Supremacy may command things for men in and of themselves, impossible to do. If God bids us to believe in Jesus Christ, and by so doing we shall have eternal life, yet it is impossible of ourselves to believe, as it is for us to make a world. Does God do well then in bidding of us to believe? If he does well (as sure he does) why do we then complain? Is not that which he wills excellent and altogether to be desired? But suppose anyone should in this way object, that although God is the Sovereign Lord over all, and may by virtue of his Sovereignty command what he will, yet whether or not he does command anything contrary to reason? So the Objection says, to command impossibilities, is to command things unreasonable.

First, I will *answer*,

That there is a great difference between God's reason (if I may use such an expression) and ours. We reason either carnally, or as at best, according to the Law of reason, or that reason which we see in the Law. But God's reason, or the reason *in* God, which moved him to give us a law, is either from himself, or ends in himself. The reason that was in God to give us a Law is one thing, and the reason that is in that Law, or that the law works in us is another, and yet both helps to clear God in this business. It is God's reason to give us a Law, and his Law is good, and yet we through our unreasonableness break this reasonable Law. I hope we will neither blame God or his Law. It is corrupt reason that will quarrel against the will of God, true reason will never. If a Master commands a servant to do any unreasonable thing, he does ill, because he is to follow the law of reason in all his commands, but God cannot command any unreasonable thing, because his will is the highest reason. There is reason in his law, and yet his will is more reasonable, (if we may so speak), for the cause is greater than the effect, and his will is the cause of his Law.

But secondly, true reason will help us to clear God in this thing, and says much more, reason will make God the highest cause, and not only the highest cause, but also the ground and procurer of all causes and things whatsoever. And if this is so, then he must be the Supreme Lord over all, and if Supreme, then reason will tell us, that he may command what he will. Indeed, if a master commands a servant to do things impossible, he does ill, because there is a command laid on the master that he ought not to oppress his servant, and therefore reason will tell us that he does ill. But there is no reason that can tell us, either that God is tied to the observation of any particular command, or that he is limited or strengthened in the commanding of such and such particular things beyond which he ought not to pass: But true reason will tell us that he may command what he will, and if he commands that which does please him, then he is just and righteous. If God can give himself a reason to satisfy himself, why he gives such and such a Law, and if we by reason can satisfy ourselves, that if he pleases, he may give such a Law, then if he is pleased, *why do we complain?* Suppose God should command any man to make a world, (I only put it by way of supposition) I would ask that man whether God does well or not in so doing. I am confident when he commands men to believe, he bids them to do a thing equivalent to making the world, for the works require one and the same power to bring forth these things to light. But we are apt to quarrel against God, because his ways are above our ways, but if it were not so, how could he be God.

We may be brought higher and higher by degrees into the knowledge of the glory of God, and the surpassing excellency of his eternal being: but it cannot be imagined, that he should stoop below himself, to portray himself suitable to the model of our carnal apprehensions.

It is true God does stoop low, but never below himself, for God to stoop low is this, that through the height of his goodness and grace he is pleased to discover something of that divine and everlasting invisible excellence, which is treasured up within his own breast. But to stoop below himself (I mean in a strict sense) is to lose the height of that goodness and grace, and to make himself appear to be something that he is not, which is not to be thought. For God cannot delude, which he must do, if he should *appear* to be that which he is *not*. Therefore, if we know that God speaks *thus and thus*, or bids us to do *such and such* things, when we by the weakness of our capacity, cannot fathom his way, then let us sit down and say, "O! How unsearchable is his wisdom, and his ways past finding out."

Thus have I briefly treated about the nature of Adam's fall, or the means and way by which he came to fall. If I knew any other *Objection* of any concernment that might arise, I should endeavour to answer it.

*FINIS.*

# IMPRIMATUR: SERMON 3

*Die Mercurii* 24. April, 1644.

It is this day ordered by the Commons assembled in Parliament, that Sir Robert Harley and Sir Robert Pye do from this House give thanks to Doctor Stanton and Master Greene, for the great pains they took in the sermons they preached this day at St. Margaret's Westminster at the entreaty of this House, it being the day of public Humiliation. And they are desired to print their sermons. And it is ordered that none shall presume to print either of their sermons, but by the authority of their hands writing.

*H. Elsyng. Cler. Parl. D. Com.*

---

I appoint *Philemon Stephens* to print my sermon,
*John Greene.*

# NEHEMIAH'S TEARS

[ORIGINAL TITLE PAGE]

## NEHEMIAH'S
Tears and Prayers
FOR
## JUDAH'S AFFLICTION,
And the ruins and repair of
## JERUSALEM.

Delivered in a SERMON in the Church
Of Magaret's Westminster, before the Honorable
House of Commons upon the Day of their Monthly
Humiliation, *April* 24, 1644.

---

BY
## JOHN GREENE
Master of Arts, Late Pastor of
*Pencomb* in the County of *Hereford.*

---

Isaiah 22:4, 9, "*Look away from me, I will weep bitterly, labor not to comfort me, because of the spoiling of the daughter of my people. Ye have seen also the breeches of the city of David, that they are many.*"

Psalm 51:18, "*Do good in thy good pleasure unto Zion: build thou the walls of Jerusalem.*"

---

*LONDON*
Printed by *G.M* for *Philemon Stephens*, and are to be sold at his
Shop at the golden Lion in *Paul's Church-yard.*
1644.

PIISSIMO,
PRUDENTISSIMO,
AMPLISSIMOQUE SENATUI
DOMUS COMMUNIUM
IN PARLIAMENTO,

CLEMENTISSIMA DEI
PROVIDENTIA CONVOCATO,
POTENTISSIMA DEI TUTELA
CONTINUATO,

MEDITATIUNCULAS HAS SUAS
TENUICULAS JUSSU è SUGGESTO
EDITAS, HORTATU VESTRO
TYPIS EVALGATAS,

HONORIS ET OBSERVANTIAE
ERGO
SUMMA CUM HUMILITATE
D. O. V.

Amplitudini vestrae in Domino obsequentissimus,

*John Greene.*

[*Most gracious and prudent senate, those of the common parliament, before the merciful God, the one who calls providence into being, as it has been given by order of the pulpit editor, to your encouragement, honor and respect, we therefore stress, in greatest humility, to print this sermon.*
*Humbly,*
*John Greene*]

# THE SERMON

A SERMON PREACHED Before the Honorable House of COMMONS at their Monthly Fast on *April*, 24, 1644.

Nehemiah 1:3-4, "And they said unto me, The remnant that are left of the captivity there in the province are in great affliction and reproach: the wall of Jerusalem also is broken down, and the gates thereof are burned with fire. And it came to pass, when I heard these words, that I sat down and wept, and mourned certain days, and fasted, and prayed before the God of heaven."

The first verse of the words read (if you look back to the next before; Nehemiah 1:1) are the answer of Hanani and certain men of Judah unto a question moved by Nehemiah, being then in Shushan the Palace, the winter house of the Kings of Persia:[18] Josephus[19] relates the story as thus: Nehemiah meeting certain strangers entering the gates of the City Shushan, perceiving them to have come a long journey, and hearing them speaking one to another in the Hebrew tongue, he demanded of them where they came, answering that they came out of Judea, he puts a two-fold question to

---

[18] Lavater ex Athenco, lib. 12. cap. 30.
[19] Antiquitat. lib. 10. cap. 5.

them: one, it stood with the people of the Jews, that were returned out of the captivity, and then in the province of Judea; the other, what was the condition of Jerusalem. And in the former words of the text they give answer to both (and it was a sad answer) for the Jews that came out of the captivity, they are in a very miserable condition, in great affliction and reproach, under many hard pressures, full of scorn and contempt, and for Jerusalem it remains still in its old ruins, the walls continue to be broken down, the gates burnt with fire; and if we shall add to these the time when this report was made, which will appear by comparing the first verse of this Chapter with the first of the second (Nehemiah 1:1 and 2:3), to have been in the twentieth year of Artexerxes the King, we have, as I conceive, the sum of that which the former verse holds out.

In the latter you may see how this sad report affected Nehemiah, it put him also into a sad condition, when he heard how it was with people, how with Jerusalem, he wept and mourned, and it was not a little sudden melancholic fit for a time, but it held out certain days; and to show that this mourning of his was real, did really affect him, that it came indeed from bowels of pity and compassion towards the people and the city, it put him upon those means, that (if any) would minister relief to the city and the people, and make way for their freedom from former pressures, and expedite the repair of present ruins: And these are two, he fasted and he prayed, and in the latter you may consider unto whom he prays, to the God of heaven, if you look to the last verse of this chapter, you shall find Nehemiah's main request was to the King, that he might find favour in his sight. His suit was to a man on earth (so he called him in that verse, *this man*) yet he goes to heaven for obtaining it, as knowing it would avail him little to go to the King, unless he went first to God to move the King's heart. He had a final hope that his petition could speed with man, but not until it was first presented to God.

Here is ground you see, for a variety of observations, I shall do, as you use, when you go to a shop furnished with a choice of several wares, you will not take *all* that may be had, but only such as best fits your occasions. So shall I by God's assistance out of this variety, observable from the text, endeavour to single out what I conceive will best suit with our present times and somewhat further the duties of this day.

You shall hear the Lord before the Captivity making a gracious promise by the Prophet Jeremiah to the people of the Jews; when 70 years are accomplished at Babylon, "I will visit you and perform my good word towards you, in causing you to return to this place, for I know the thoughts, that I think towards you, says the Lord, thoughts of peace, and not of evil, to give you an expected end," (Jeremiah 29:10-11). Here was a precious *promise* made before they knew the misery, that should make them stand in need of such a promise. And the Lord began to make this good, when in the first year of Cyrus, according to the Promise, "the Lord stirred up the spirit of Cyrus by Proclamation to grant free liberty unto all the people, to go up unto Jerusalem, and to build the Temple," (Ezra 1:1-3). And if you go to the fifth verse, you shall see how fairly the work proceeded, "The Lord stirred up also the spirits of the chiefs of the fathers of Judah, and Benjamin, and the Priests, and the Levites, with all them whose spirit God had raised, to go up, to build the house of the Lord, which is in Jerusalem."

And yet many years after (as you shall hear in the following passages) comes this sad report to Nehemiah, that all was at a stand for Jerusalem, "The remnant of the people that are left were in great affliction and reproach. the wall of the city remained broken down, and the gates thereof burnt with fire."

An expected end God had promised, and questionless ,the people of the Jews had long looked for the accomplishment of this promise, but it must not come yet, they had more affliction to suffer, the walls of Jerusalem must remain longer in their ruins, and the gates in their ashes.

So we shall find the Lord often dealing with his Church and people, they seldom enjoy any great blessing, or enter on the fruition of any special promised mercy, but it costs them dear. God made a promise to Abraham, that he would give him and his posterity that goodly land of Canaan (Genesis 15:7), yet they must pay dear for this before they had it, "Know of a surety, [God says] that thy seed shall be a stranger in a land that is not theirs, and they shall serve them, and they shall afflict them four hundred years," (Genesis 15:13). They must not look to have so pleasant and fruitful a land for nothing; no it must cost them dear, many years of hard service, a great deal of affliction, they must go through an, "iron furnace," (Deuteronomy 4:20), so is Egypt called, represented (as it may seem) to Abraham in his vision in that, "smoking furnace," (Genesis 15:17). Another instance may be that of Joseph, who was assured that he should have the honor which his dreams had promised (Genesis 37:5-9), but it must cost him his being sold for a servant, his casting in prison, his feet hurt with fetters, he was laid in iron (Psalm 105:17-18), or as the margent, his soul came into iron, and here he was brought into a far lower condition then he was at the time of his dreams, yet see the over-ruling providence of the most wise God so disposing, that every descent into a lower condition, was made to him as a stair to ascend to that honor which his dreams had promised.[20]

---

[20] *Divino judeto qual deoderare conatisunt rearendo serverunt, Greg. Moral. L.6. c 8t. Deo vendixus est a raeibus Joseph nealoraretur sedided est adoratus quia venditus, sic diverum consitiumdun devitatur impletur sic bumanasaptentia dua retuctatur comprehendatur ld. bib.*

To come nearer to ourselves, and that which concerns the Church, this latter age of the world, there was a glorious Promise made to the Church by that Evangelical Prophet, "I say, Behold, I create a new heavens, and a new earth, and the former shall not be remembered, nor come into mind. But be you glad and rejoice forever, in that which I create," (Isaiah 65:17-19). And John the *Prophetical Evangelist* gives the Church such assurance as this, as if he had then seen it performed, "I saw a new heaven and a new earth, for the first heaven and the first earth were passed away. And I John saw the holy city, the new Jerusalem coming down from God out of heaven," (Revelation 21:1-4). And the Church expects the accomplishment hereof, "We [the Apostle says] according to his Promise, look for new heavens, and a new earth, in which dwelleth righteousness," (2 Peter 3:13). It is now the Church's expectation, we look with John to see this new heaven, and new earth, and to behold that holy City coming down from Heaven, we hope the Lord at this present is about this work. But go back to the former part of this prophecy, and you shall find, that the Church must not have this new heaven and new earth, until it has paid dear for them, you may see from the eighth chapter to this 21$^{st}$, what the Church paid for this before she had it. I will instance only in the 12th and 13$^{th}$ chapters, in the former you have the great red dragon, that is, as our best interpreters take it, the Devil, and what mischief he did to the Church, you may find in several passages of that chapter, he stood before the woman, which was to be delivered. For to devour her child as soon as it was born, not being able to devour the child, he persecuted the woman which brought forth the man child, casting out of his mouth water as a flood after the woman, that he might cause her to be carried away by the flood, and when no prevailing against her, he went to make war with the remnant of her seed, which keep the commandments of God and have the testimony of Jesus Christ (Revelation 12:3-4, 13, 15, 17).

In the next chapter there is one beast rising out of the sea, having seven heads and ten horns, the heathenish Roman Empire, "And to him it was given to make war with the Saints, and to overcome them", verse 7, in verse eleven, there is another beast rising out of the earth, the Papacy, which had the power of the first beast, and did by many lying wonders deceive them that dwell on the earth; what the Church has suffered by the cruelty and subtlety of these two beasts, the histories of the Church do abundantly manifest. It cost the Primitive times the tortures and blood of many thousands of martyrs before truth and peace settled by Constantine and Theodosius. I do not need to tell you of what our own Kingdom, Germany and France paid for the beginning of the Reformation.

If you would have my thoughts, why the Lord in his wisdom sells his choice mercies at so dear a rate, I conceive it may be, 1. To try what esteem his Church has of those mercies it looks for; the Church of God in all places expects great mercies, we of this land at this time look for special favours, we look for the Reformation of what is amiss in Church and State, for an establishment of Truth and Peace, the Lord now would try how we esteem these, how we prize them, what we are willing to part for the enjoyment of them, we will not give much for that which we value so little, large offers argue a high esteem. God is now trying the hearts of England, great matters are expected, but how do we prize them? Surely it cannot be better known, then by what we will give for the purchase of them. Will we part with all to enjoy them? Do we think our whole estates, our children, our nearest friends, our dearest blood not too dear a price to pay for them? It is as undoubted evidence, that we highly prize those things which we neither will nor can want whatsoever they cost us, when all that we have, and more if we had it, shall freely go for them, and questionless, that wise merchant could no way so fully manifest his esteem of the pearl to be more worth than all he had, then when he sold all that he had, and bought it. (Matthew 13:46).

The Lord does this to work a greater esteem of these mercies, when he is pleased to bestow them. Health is much prized by all, but more by those that have lain many years upon the bed of languishing. Liberty is sweet to and desirable of all, but most of those that have known the hardship of a long imprisonment; the violence and danger of a storm makes a safe harbour the more welcome. The diseased woman that was cured of her issue of twelve years continuance, would have taken it for a great favour, if any of the physicians she made use of could have cured her, but when she had spent all, and found herself not the better, but the worse, then Christ to come and heal her without any further cost or pains but only the touch of the hem of his garment, could not but work in her greater and more thankful esteem of her cure (Mark 5:25-27). The impotent man at the pool at Bethesda, that had an infirmity thirty eight years, would have been very glad if any man would have helped him into the water, when the angel troubled it, and it was his complaint to Christ to come and heal him with a word, it could not but work in him a high esteem of that comfortable healing (John 5:3-7). Abraham much desired a child, and so desired, that when God told him, "I am thy exceeding great reward," he replies, "Alas, Lord, what wilt thou give me, seeing I go childless?" (Genesis 15:1-2) as if all God could do for him was nothing, until God gave him a child. The Lord did at length give him a child, but it was when Abraham and Sarah were out of all hope, and see how this affected both of their hearts. The text says, Abraham laughed at the promise, he grew to such an excess of joy, that he could not contain himself from laughter (Genesis 17:17). and Sarah, when the Promise was made good, and Isaac was born, "God [she says] hath made me to laugh," (Genesis 21:6, 8-9). Though her former laughter proceeded from unbelief, yet this from joy; and to show the height of joy, whereunto this mercy had raised them, their son must bear the name of their joy, be called Isaac, that is, "Laughter", Genesis 21:3.[21]

It is ordinary with us, what costs little, we do not usually esteem much, and we can easily part with it; our common Proverb, "Lightly come, lightly go." But such an estate, such a house that cost me so many thousands to purchase, so much in building, so much in furnishing, and other accommodations for my content, so that I laid out my whole estate, no, hazarded my life in running through some dangers to compass it, what, *part with this*? No, I will rather part with my life then forgo this. Surely, I am persuaded, that Reformation, just liberties, and privileges, with other mercies we now expect, if the Lord is please to give to us our expected end; or if this favour denied to us, yet vouchsafed to our posterity, I am persuaded (I say) that we and they will far more prize and esteem these by how much more they cost our

---

[21] *Referat pater admirans in gaudio riserat & mater dubitans in gaudio, sed fide confirmatarisimme non al irridendum opprobrium sed ad celebrandum gaudium pertinebar.* Aug. de. Civ. Dei, .18lc.31.

forefathers and ourselves such loss in estates, and so much blood that has been spilt to purchase and obtain them at God's hand. Is not then that done for these things, and peace which we *expect*, and for which we have long prayed, yes, and paid much also, surely it is to be feared, and we may probably conceive, that we are not yet come to God's price. England and Ireland must both bid more and abide more, before they enter upon those great desired mercies. Has it cost us much more, suppose our whole estates, no, our lives, yet that pearl in the Gospel, the Kingdom of God in its power and purity will prove more worth than all.

It is a wonder to see too many hazarding the loss of heaven to leave a great uncertain estate to their posterity on earth, and shall we think much at the cost of our purses, no, our lives, if God calls for them, to leave unto a Kingdom, to a Church, to succeeding ages a more clear and prevailing way and means to that immortal inheritance, that is prepared and reserved for the Saints in Heaven.

Soldiers will never grudge the hazard of limbs, of life, so they may get the victory, and what should dishearten or dismay any whose hearts the Lord has inclined to further the work in hand, willingly and cheerfully to lay out themselves, and what they have in their power, by which they may help the Lamb to overcome, and to set Christ on his throne, that this and all the Kingdoms of the earth may be his, who is the King of kings, and Lord of lords.

It is storied of Epaminondas, that having received by a spear his death's wound in the battle between the Thebans and Lacedemonins, the spear head remained in the wound until he heard that his army had gotten the victory, and then he rejoicingly commanded it to be plucked out, his blood and life issuing forth together, with these words, "*Sat vixi, invictus enim moriar,* I have lived long enough that die unconquered." And being told a little before his death, that however he had lost his life, yet his shield was safe, he cries out by way of exulting, "*Vester Epaminondas cum fic moritur, non moritur,* your Empaminondas thus dying, doth not die."[22]

There is no shield in life other than that of faith (Ephesians 6:16), and if the heart is right he may die with comfort in that cause, which preserves life in the doctrine of faith, leaving that safe and entire. Oh tell me, is it not an estate well weakened, that strengthens the power of Religion? Is it not a life well lost, that helps to save the life of truth? And yet a life so lost (if we dare take Christ's Word) is not lost, but saved, "Whosoever shall lose his life for my sake, and the Gospel's, shall save it," (Mark 8:35). since then we hear what God's people have paid for such mercies as we expect, if we

---

[22] *Aemilias Picha in vita be paminonde.*

have not here received what we desire; let us think, we are not yet come to that price which God looks for, and which these great mercies cost before we have them.

Again, when the Lord was about the raising up and employing good Nehemiah for perfecting the work of the Courts of the Temple, and repairing the ruins of the city Jerusalem, had that which was already done cost the people much affliction, many sufferings, and does there yet come a sad report of the low, afflicted and despised condition of the Jews then in Judea, let the consideration hereof help to support the spirits of God's people in their most sad dejecting times. you have heard there is a new heaven and new earth promised, Jerusalem to come down from heaven, a glorious building going up. And you know they which build large and great houses, being to set them on hollow and false grounds (as we call it) are forced to dig very deep before they lay the foundation. When we see this, we presently conclude, here is some great building, a frame of more than ordinary weight to be set up. I hope this is the Church's present case; it has been brought very low in Germany, in Ireland, in our own land, and we trust the Lord is in all this while digging the foundation. This is the work the Lord suffers the Church's enemies to labor in, to prepare the groundwork for erecting in his Church a glorious fabric, that these at the worst shall be but the Lord's mattocks and spades, and if the Lord be still pleased to continue them at their work in Ireland, in England, it is to be feared, that it may be, too many of the Irish hearts are yet to God-ward as rotten and hollow as their bogs, and we in England, though we have firmer ground, yet I doubt as false hearts, a great deal of hypocrisy, hollowness, and rottenness remaining, so that the Lord, though he has already gone very deep, brought us low, is not yet come to firm ground, so he may go on to bring us lower in our affliction, to work us lower in our humiliation.

And I could wish our spirits in regard of humiliation always follow as our condition, that when God throws us on the ground, we would lie on the ground, put our mouths in the dust. But at no time to be low in distrust, for our confidence in God, to have highest spirits in lowest estates, as knowing that our raising up is then at hand. If a stranger is one that never heard of the ebbing and flowing of the sea, and should come to your river, the Thames, at an high water, and should stay and observe how much it falls in six or seven hours, he might probably think that your river would run itself dry; whereas you that are acquainted with your tides, know that when your ebb is at the lowest, the tide of rising water is returning, and trust unto it the lowest estate of the Church is mostly an immediate forerunner of its raising; the Church in the Primitive times found it thus, the most raging and violent of those ten bloody Persecutions was that of

Dioclesian[23], never the like tortures invented and executed, nor so many martyred and banished, only in Egypt 144,000, put to death, 700,000 banished, yes so violent his rage that his wife Serena[24] (however a well deserving Lady) was put to death, because a Christian; but this cruelty and rage of his followed with the mild and peaceable times of Constantius, the father of Constantine the son. And it is the Lord's promise that it shall be thus, and that upon a right and religious observation of days, of fasting and humiliation, "Is not this the fast that I have chosen, to loose the bands of wickedness?" and in the close of verse 10, "then shall thy light rise in obscurity, and thy darkness be as the noon day," (Isaiah 58. 6-10), the darkest and saddest night of calamity shall be followed with a gladsome and comfortable morning of joy, so cleared from after-clouds of sorrow and distress, as is the Sun at noon day, when it shines in its fullest strength (Psalm 30:5).

To proceed, are the walls of Jerusalem broken down, and her gates burnt with fire? Jerusalem that had outstood so many sieges, from before which the confident, potent, and numerous army of Sennacherib was forced to rise and retreat with shame and loss of 85,000 in one night (Isaiah 37:36, 37), of whom the Psalmist sung after that deliverance as some think, or as others after that from that combination of those many Kings that came against Jehoshaphat (2 Chronicles 20),

---

[23] *Osiander Cent. 4. Cap. 5. Serbus Calvi., anno Christi, 8.*
[24] *Osiander Cent. 4. Cp. 9. Idem Cent 4. Cap 14. & 31.*

"Compass about Zion, go round about, and tell the towers, mark well the walls thereof, behold her bulwarks," (Psalm 48:12, 13), see if a stone is shaken, or a turf is fallen in her outworks? What Jerusalem, "She was the princess among the nations," (Lamentations 1:1), so strong, so populous, as twenty hundred thousand in it at the beginning of the siege, or as some above four million[25]; in so seeming secure a condition, as the Kings of the earth, and all the inhabitants of the world would not have believed that the enemy should enter into the gates of Jerusalem (Lamentations 4:12); the walls of this Jerusalem broken down, and her gates burnt with fire?

O learn that former deliverances will not secure sinful Kingdoms, and sinning Cities from after dangers and ruins; I will only commend unto you the instance of Nineveh made secure by the Lord's turning away a former threatened judgement, and within 40 days of execution, yet then exposed to miserable ruin, "Art thou better than populous, *No?*" from verse 8 to the end of the chapter (Nahum 3:8,9), a fit resemblance in many particulars of this land of ours, the Lord grant we may neither be like that in sin, or destruction.

And it is the desire of my soul, that this city honored here with safety, with the discovery and defeat of so many plots and attempts would seriously lay this to heart, that

---

[25] *Calvisius ex Josepho.*

former deliverances might not beget security, but more watchfulness, both to drive out those sins which are the apparent in-lets to an enemy, and to discover and prevent the secret contrivances of falsehearted brethren, considering the continued vigilancy and unsatiable rage of the Church's enemies, and specially of your city. The fenced cities that belonged to Judah would not satisfy Shishack the King of Egypt (2 Chronicles 12:4), but he came up against Jerusalem, the likes of Sennacherib (Isaiah 36:1, 2). The same is certainly said of the enemy's malice and fury against your city, and I think I hear the General's saying of yours, as once Ahab of Ramoth in Gilead, *Know ye not that London is ours, and be we still, and take it not out of the hands of Rebels and traitors?* (1 Kings 22:3) (for so they call you) or as Haman once said of Mordecai, all the honor and favour I enjoy avails me nothing, so long as I see Mordecai the Jew sitting in the King's gate (Esther 5:13). That they have Bristol in the West, York in the North, with others, will not satisfy, unless they had London also. And believe it, their taking of other places, is but to make way for the surprise of this. You shall observe a workman sent into rough woods for the chopping down of some great oak tree beset with briars or smaller shrubs, first cutting up these; but for what end? Surely that nothing might stand in his way, which might hinder his full stroke at the oak to cut that down, so assuredly their taking of what other places so ever, is but to make way for their full (and if they could reach it) fatal blow against this City.

As therefore to raise up your hearts to great thankfulness, we may say of your City, as they of Laish, It is, "a place where there is no want of anything in the earth," (Judges 18:10), so I beseech you, do not let that be said of you, which was of them in a former verse, they, "saw the people that were therein, how they dwelt careless, quiet and secure," (Judges 18:7). And no greater provocations to an attempt, then wealth and security, the Danites presently set on them (Judges 18:9, 11-12); let therefore the enemy's rage and vigilance for your ruin, double your circumspection, and increase the firmer union of hearts affections and endeavours for your preservation.

To go yet further in the report, when did it come to Nehemiah? It was (as you heard) in the twentieth year of Artaxerxes the King, as our best Chronologers compute, about 146 years after their return from Babylon.[26] So slowly, for the most part, go up the repairs of God's people, not alone in the Civil, but Ecclesiastic state, the Temple whose foundation laid the second year after their return, not finished until 111 years after, in the 6th year of Darius, and for the Temple-Service and Worship, Reformation of many things

---

[26] Calvisius, & allis.

concerning the Sabbath, teaching the Law, and rebuilding the gates of the Courts of the Temple, were not done until after this time by Ezra and Nehemiah (Ezra 3:6, 8, 15). It was in this way in primitive times, Philip, the first heathenish Emperor that was baptized, began some Reformation in the year of Christ 247[27]. Constantine went on where Philip left in the year 310. Theodosius 395 added what Constantine had omitted; so Reformation, then a 150 years, was not growing to any great measure of perfection.

Several reasons might be given why the Temple and City work went on so slowly in Jerusalem, I shall entreat you to take notice of the most remarkable.

The first, the violent oppositions of Jerusalem's enemies, (and we never find any good work begun for the welfare of Church and State, which the power and policy of Hell did not oppose.), "It grieved exceedingly Sanballat the Horonite, and Tobiah the servant of the Ammonite, that there was come a man to seek the welfare of the children of Israel," (Nehemiah 2:10). And in these enemies, we may consider first their quality men of place and command, Rehum the Chancelor, or as Tremellius reads it, *Prases Concilii*, President of the Council, one that ruled the Councel Tables, and Shimshai the Scribe, or as in the Margent, the Secretary, or as Tremellius, *Legis peritus* the Lawyer (Ezra 4:8); and to their

---

[27] Osiander.

assistance came Tatnai the Governor, or as the Geneva, the Captain and his Companions (Ezra 5:3), and to make them a square number, a quaternion, you shall find Noadiah the Prophetess (Nehemiah 6:14) (the female sex will be stirring) and other false Prophets appearing against the work, and the persons employed in it, and surely when any good work is intended or begun for the Church and State, it would be a wonder, and the devil might seem much to forget himself, if he should not make use of some ill affected, or disaffected Churchmen to hinder and oppose it.

I will not stay you with their methods, by engaging the Kings of Persia in the opposition, by procuring Edicts and Letters, and Proclamations against them, and that on false informations of rebellion, sedition, not paying tribute, custom, and endamaging the King's revenue (Ezra 4:12, 13); nor will I trouble with their manner of opposing, by scoffs against their persons and their work (Nehemiah 2:19), by combinations to take up arms, to hinder the work by the sword, and by hire to corrupt some of those that sided with Nehemiah, either to betray him, or to put him on some dishonorable or hazardous attempt, all these are obvious to every eye that will but read the story, and I presume you often hear of them (Nehemiah 4:2, 3, 8; Nehemiah 6:10, 12). so that whether you consider the variety of the opposers, like Samson's foxes turned tail to tail and firebrands between them (Judges 15:4)[28] (and I am sure the Scripture affords some of them no better names) (Isaiah 9:15) an affeciation of Courtiers, Lawyers, Soldiers, false prophets; or their drawing in Kings to countenance, protect and authorize them, or lastly, all their Methods and proceedings, you may discern our times so paralleling those, as if the present plot were drawn from theirs, and the model fetched from there.

A second reason may be the smallness of the number that returned unto Judea and Jerusalem, but one of six, two tribes of twelve, Judah and Benjamin, and whether all of these a question, their whole number with men and maid-servants under 50, 000 (Nehemiah 7:67) and those that did return, so much minding their own houses, the repair of their own ruins, as the Temple and Jerusalem was neglected, so the Prophet, "Is it time for you, O ye, to dwell in your ceiled houses, and this house lie waste?" (Haggai 1:4).

What great hinderances have private interests been to the public good, the breaches of Jerusalem less minded, because too many, too much mind their own, "My house, saith the Lord, is waste, and why, ye run every man to his own house?" (Haggai 1:9). It was that which kept Asher from joining with Deborah and Barak against Sisera; "Asher continued on the Sea shore, and abode in his breaches,"

---

[28] Song of Songs 3:15.

(Judges 5:17), he dwelt in a sea-town much decayed, had suffered already by the enemy, and so had enough to do, to make up and make good his own breaches; Don Alfonso King of Aragon, was accustomed to say, that if he had been Emperor when Rome flourished, he would have built a Temple before the Capital, in which the Senators should lay down all private interests, and lay aside their own particular benefits whenever anything was to be done for the weak public, before they went to crave assistance of their gods[29]; And surely it is great pity, that any man's private respect should hinder the common good; nor will it be all with the body politic, where it is not with this as natural, which will willingly loose a great deal of blood in some vein, many times to fainting, will endure the cutting off a limb or two to preserve the health and life of the whole.

And here give me leave to commend to all, (whose hearts and desires the Lord has stirred up to further the public good) these two short directions. 1. So seriously to mind the public good, as if in respect of what they minded nothing else; and secondly, to go about the public work with united minds, see the fruit of these two, both for Temple and State-work in the story of Ezra and Nehemiah (Ezra 3:1), how speedily went up the Altar and foundation of the temple, when the people

---

[29] Fr. Ch. de Fonseca.

gathered themselves as one man to Jerusalem. And for the city's repair, "So built we the wall, and all the wall was joined together unto the half thereof:" and he will tell you what caused this, "the people had a mind to work," (Nehemiah 4:6), a mind and union of minds, what will they not compass?

The greatest number, even ten parts of twelve chose rather to stay in Babylon to support that, and keep their estates there, than return into Judea, and afford their help for rebuilding Jerusalem; And are there not too many that would willingly prop and keep up tottering Romish Babylon? Too few whose hearts are real to repair the decays of spiritual Jerusalem, whereas if we cordially desire that Jerusalem may go up, we must in good earnest endeavour that Babylon may come down, for certainly Jerusalem will never be in its beauty, while Babylon is in her pride.[30] And would we have encouragement to pull down Babylon, what greater, then that of the Psalmist, which will as truly be versified of Babylon in Italy; as once of Babylon in Chaldea, "Babylon, who art to be destroyed," (Psalm 137:8;. and this so certain, as an Angel near 1600 years ago, spoke of it, as already down, "Babylon the great is fallen, is fallen," (Revelation 18:2), and the time of her fall is we hope so near, as I think I hear the Lord summoning all the parts of his Church throughout the world against Romish Babylon, as once against that other, "Put yourselves in

[30] Calvis. Anno Christi, 95.

array against Babylon round about, all ye that bend the bow, shoot to her, spare no arrows. for she hath sinned against the Lord," (Jeremiah 50:14). Let me, I pray you have your leave and audience to press this with some enlargement.

The Lord long ago foretold, that those ten horns, which had formerly given their power to the whore, should hate the whore, and shall not all be willing and ready to do that (Revelation 17:17), which God will have done, but must we go no farther, than to hate her, yes, this hatred must carry us on to the use of all means to make her desolate, and naked; but why hate her and shoot at her? Because she seeks our lives, plunders us of our estates, bereaves us of our peace? No look at the close of the verse in the Prophet, "for she hath sinned against the Lord," robbing in most of her doctrines, God of his glory, Christ of his honor.

The bow and arrows were in former ages the glory of our Nation, many glorious victories gotten by our English archers, never a more sure need for them to appear then now, and the Lord now if he ever calls for them, and there is none in this Congregation from the greatest to the least, but God has given him a bow and arrow with it that he may shoot against Babylon.

Your bow, noble and worthy Patriots, is the power which God, your just Privileges and the Laws of this Land have put into your hands, it is a bow of steel, and I hope the strongest arm of flesh shall never be able to break it. You have a quiver full of precious and piercing arrows, your wisdom, vigilance, faithfulness, zeal, courage, your votes, orders, ordinances, and which is the strength of all, your blessed unanimity; the moral of Scylurus the Scythian King,[31] his 80 arrows given to his 80 sons at his death, is I am persuaded well known, and I desire may be always thought on, no strength being able to break them, while bound up, and bundled together in the sheaf; the Lord give you Joseph's blessing and you, as he, have need of it, "The Archers have sorely grieved him, and shot at him and hated him," (Genesis 49:23, 24); is not your condition like this? Are not you those against whom the workers of iniquity, "bend their bows, to shoot their arrows, even bitter words?" (Psalm 64. 2-5). But this bow abode in strength, and the arms of his hands were made strong, by the hands of the mighty God of Jacob; The Lord also be pleased to give you all a double portion of Job's honor, "My glory [*he says*] was fresh in me, and my bow was renewed in my hand," (Job 29:20), that is, say some, let my power and authority be never diminished, let me not err in judgement, let all my counsels be directed and prospered by the Lord[32], or as others, let there be a daily increase of my strength, to pass through all oppositions, and to overcome all

---

[31] Plutarch. Merat. *De garrutitate.*
[32] Pineda.

difficulties[33], and the Lord keep that in the Psalm far from everyone of you, "They turned back and dealt unfaithfully, they were turned aside like a broken bow?" (Psalm 78:57).

Those to whom the Lord has given ability of body, their bow and arrow is their strength, let them put out that, offer themselves willingly, not need a press, much less hide themselves from a press, God's people, whenever God has need of them are a willing people; volunteers in God's service are always best accepted, "My heart is towards the governors of Israel, which offered themselves willingly," (Judges 5:9), it would be very pleasing unto God, if that might be found in them in the literal sense, which the Psalmist otherwise applies, "Thy people shall come willingly at the time of assembling thine army," (Psalm 110:3), so the Geneva translation reads it, and know you can never more honor God with your strength, than by joining with those that fight the battles of this strong Lord against Babylon.

You to whom the Lord has given wealth and estates, your bow and arrow is your purse, do not spare his, do not say you have given or lent much already, and hope you may be now excused. And rather, because you fear all you have given is lost, and for your parts, here is such daily calling for further Contributions and loans, as you do not know, what is best to

---

[33] Mercerus.

do, give me leave to tell you what I conceive will be best, do not let God's cause want while you have ability to give, do not let that arrow which you may shoot, be hid in the quiver when God calls for it. And if you think all is lost that has been formerly given, do as those which having shot two or three arrows, which they think are lost, they will, so near as they can, shoot towards the same place one or two arrows after the former to find them out, you do not know whether what you give or lend now to further the present expedition, may not by God's blessing be a means to bring in with advantage what has been already given, or to preserve what is left, if neither of these, yet O the comfort that this will one day bring unto your consciences, when you can truly say, God gave me a great estate, and I thank my God, with comfort I can speak it, and I bless his Name for it, he gave me a heart, not to see his cause at any time want, what I had to give. Let me commend a worthy pattern to you, of David and the chief of the fathers, the captains of thousands and hundreds, and it was for Temple work, and they offered largely, "Then the people rejoiced for that they offered willingly, because with a perfect heart they offered willingly to the Lord, and David the King also rejoiced with great joy," (1 Chronicles 29:6, 7, 9).

But it may be, here is many an aged, a weak, a poor man, no women and children, that have good hearts to be shooting against Babylon, if we could find a bow and arrow that they were able to deal with, yes, I can fit you all, even the weakest arm in the Congregation, I shall commend a bow to you. Which if used aright will be as successful, as the bow of Jonathan, that does not turn back from the blood of the slain, from the fat of the mighty (2 Samuel 1:22), it is the bow of prayer, the ejaculations of a holy heart, shot up to heaven, these arrows have steel heads, they will pierce and stick where they hit, sharp and keen in the heart of the enemy, they are invisible arrows, the enemy can neither discover nor decline them, they will kill in the dark, this arrow will find a joint in Ahab's armor (1 Kings 22:34), draw this arrow as Jehu did against Jehoram with your full strength, and doubt not but it will in God's time smite our Romish Jehoram at the heart, and sink him in his Chariot and chair of pride (2 Kings 9:24); O that whenever our armies are in the field charging the enemy, shower of these arrows of fervent prayers, a volley of this shot might light as thick on the enemy's camp, as those hailstones at Beth-horon (Joshua 10:11), we should, I do not doubt, see more slain by this shower of prayer than the sword.

Are the walls of Jerusalem yet broken down? It may be that which is the first work in repairing ruinous walls was not then done, the rubbish of the former decays not yet removed, and this was the people's reason and part of their complaint (Nehemiah 4:10); there is much rubbish, so that we are not able to build the wall.

I pray you lay this to heart, you that desire in any way to be repairers of our breaches, do repairs in Church and State move slowly? Let me ask, is all the rubbish of our Church and State removed? God be blessed, much is, but is there not too much remaining? No Achans in our camps, that either bear too great affection to some rags of Babylonian garments of Rome? (Joshua 7:21). Or look more after our shekels of silver, and wedges of gold; more to the pay, than an end of the war and welfare of Church and State? Is there no more drunkenness in our taverns, no falsehoods in our shops, no whoredomes in our chambers, no excess and vanity in our attire? What means that costliness and lightness in apparel, it may be, even on this day of mourning,

*Non est conveniens luctibus ille color:*

Surely sable colours will best suit with sad times, when the people mourned upon the hearing of evil tidings, "No man did put on him his ornaments," (Exodus 33:4), or as the Geneva, no man put on his best raiment.

How do I wish, that I might not justly take up that charge of the prophet against Israel, with a little variation, and that to the worse, "The pride of Israel doth testify to his face," (Hosea 5:5), too openly and manifestly declares itself in the faces of some, what means the continuance of paint, of spots, of nakedness, are not these part of that rubbish, which God says we should remove? Let me reason a little with you (if any such here) is it not better for you to remove them yourselves, than to stay until God in wrath comes to remove them? If you will not suffer yourselves to be cured by admonition, God has a cure for all these, which when it comes you cannot put off. They say there is white and red paint, O wash them off with tears of repentance, lest God bring upon you that in the Prophet, "a voice of fear and trembling, and all faces gather paleness," (Jeremiah 30:5-6), either through fear or famine. and for black spots, think a day of blackness may come too soon, in which all faces shall gather blackness (Joel 2:2, 6); hear Jeremiah lamenting this when it came upon them, "Their visage is blacker than coal," (Lamentations 4:7, 8), even theirs who were purer than the snow, and whiter than milk, and from where came this? He will tell you in the following chapter, "Our skin was black like an Oven, because of the terrible famine," (Lamentations 5:10); and for this nakedness of pride, one Prophet will tell you, that God has a, "nakedness of vengeance," (Isaiah 47:3); and he has an enemy as in another, that shall discover her nakedness, shall take, "her sons and daughters, shall slay her with the sword and execute judgement upon her," (Ezekiel 23:10).

Much other rubbish and sinks of sin might be discovered in our persons, in our families, you have Scavengers to clean your streets, well were it for your city, if there was not more filth in many houses and shops, than is cast out into the streets, happy would it be, if every master of family (pardon the word) would ply the Scavenger in his own house, in his own heart, that the inside of the platter might be made clean also (Matthew 23:26), and take we heed lest the lack of this besom of reformation, bring not on your houses the besom of destruction (Isaiah 14:23).

Lastly, are the gates of Jerusalem burnt with fire, and so continue? It may be the matter which kindled that fire is not yet removed. And will you look that a fire should go out, while the fuel remains that feeds it. What kindled the fire in the gates of Jerusalem, the Prophet will tell you, "If ye will not hearken to me, to allow the Sabbath day, and not to bear a burden, even entering in at the gates of Jerusalem on the Sabbath day; then will I kindle a fire in the gates of it, and it shall devour the palaces of Jerusalem, and it shall not be quenched (Jeremiah 17:27). And if you will go to a following Chapter of this Book, you shall find Nehemiah complaining, and charging the Nobles of Judah with this sin of the people, what evil thing is this that you do and profane the Sabbath day (Nehemiah 13:17, 18), the profanation was by them, verse 15, that trod wine-presses, and brought in sheaves on the Sabbath day, yet the Nobles not hindering it are charged with it, and all the evils brought on their fathers and the city ascribed of this sin.

They were my Meditations on the coming forth of that book for that sinful Liberty on the Lord's Day, (and I did not forbear to express them) when I too often heard in neighboring Parishes drums beating upon for a Morris or a May-pool on that day, we had just cause to fear, lest the Lord should punish that sin, with beating up the drums for a march on that day; and the Lord has brought our fears upon us, how many marches have been on that day since the beginning of these wars; I have long thought it one of the highest provoking sins of this land, and I think the Lord would have us take notice of it (as I presume many did) that leading general battle at Kineton *on the Lord's day*, could it do less then lead this Kingdom to take notice of that general leading sin, the profanation of that day? But I hope those many Ordinances for suppressing this profaneness will be a good means through God's mercy to quench our unnatural flames, if to good laws, which are the life of State, be added careful execution, which is the life of the laws.

I have done with the report, and proceed to what it wrought in Nehemiah, "And it came to pass when I hear these words, that I sat down and wept, and mourned certain days," (Nehemiah 1:4). One would think Nehemiah had little cause so to take on, at the report of the affliction of the Jews, and

Jerusalem's ruins, himself then enjoying all the honor and content that the favour of the King and the palace Shushan could afford. But alas, Gracious and Religious hearts have compassionate and tender affections, and they cannot easily put off the common miseries of God's people; the Lord himself is affected with them, that is a sweet expression in the Prophet, of the Lord's love and pity towards his people, "In all their affliction he was afflicted," (Isaiah 63:9); but that in the book of Judges is beyond expression, "His soul was grieved for the misery of Israel," (Judges 10:16), and surely there are none of the Lord's people which are not in this partakers in part of the divine nature; I cannot omit that of Isaiah, "Look away from me, I will weep bitterly, labor not to comfort me, because of the spoiling of the daughter of my people," (Isaiah 22:4). and yet this, when he did but foresee and foretell the spoiling to come. So Daniel, "mourned three whole weeks, and did eat no pleasant bread," (Daniel 10:2, 3), found no sweetness or delight in any bread or food that he took. While his brethren the Jews fed (as Isaiah expresses it), "with the bread of adversity, and the water of affliction," (Isaiah 30:20).

I do not dare adventure to give reasons why it is, and ought to be this way, I shall only entreat you, before I apply, to take notice, that there are two sorts of tears required of God's people. There is one of compassion, and another of humiliation, the former for the miseries of God's people, the

latter for the sins of God's people that brought those miseries;
both which like two streams falling into one channel met in
good Nehemiah. I might for our imitation commend several
instances of both, take one or two for the first, begin with that
of Christ, even when he rode in state and triumph towards
Jerusalem he could not behold Jerusalem, nor think of the
desolation coming upon it with dry eyes, "when he beheld the
city, he wept over it," (Luke 19:36-38, 41). Add that of Elisha,
when he did but look on Hazael, "The man of God wept. And
when Hazael said, why weepeth my lord? He answered,
Because I know the evil that thou wilt do unto the children of
Israel. their strong holds wilt thou set on fire, and their young
men wilt thou slay with the sword, and wilt dash their
children, and rip up their women with child," (2 Kings 8:11,
12).

I might acquaint you with instances of compassion,
even towards enemies, Julius Caesar pursuing Pompeii into
Egypt, there presented with Pompeii's head, wept, and at his
return to Rome, refused to triumph for that victory.[34] The
same of Charles the 5th upon his great victory over the French
King at the siege of Pavia, he strictly forbade all ringing of
bells, bon fires, or any expressions of joy for his victory,

---

[34] Imperial history, *Pedro Mexia* translated by Edward Grimstone on the life
of Julius Caesar.

because it was against Christians, though his enemies[35]; yes, even the Scythian Tamerlane, when he walked among the slain after a bloody victory against Muscovites, he accounted those Princes unhappy, which by the destruction of their own kind, sought to advance their own honor, protecting himself to be grieved even from his heart to see such sorrowful tokens of his victory.

And for tears of Humiliation, how these in the days of solemn fasting required? How the fasts of God's people recorded in his book have been watered with these (Isaiah 22:12; Joel 2:12; Judges 20:26; I Samuel 7:6; Esther 4:3), and what streams of mercy have issued from them, has been at large in a very fruitful Sermon delivered in this place, I will close both these with that of Christ's upon the Samaritan's compassion to the wounded man, "Go and do thou likewise," (Luke 10:37).

And for the first, we cannot want objects for tears of Compassion, whether we look upon the plundered, fired, and bleeding condition of our brethren in Germany, Ireland, and the most parts of our own Nation; or (which should more melt us) the lamentable soul distresses of the remoter parts of our land, those children of Wales and the Counties adjoining, in which there are many thousands, that in respect of the knowledge of God, of Christ, the way to salvation, do not

---

[35] The same in the life of Charles the 5th, Turkish history, Knokes.

know the right hand from the left; now the good Lord incline your hearts to a seasonable and speedy prosecution of that work which the Lord in mercy has begun in some of those parts.

Nor if we look into our own hearts, our families, our cities, our countries, our armies, can we want objects for tears of humiliation, causes too many for every soul, every family to mourn apart, and surely did our land weep more for sin, it would bleed less; tears are the souls blood, did these run as they ought, they might help to stay or turn the issue of blood in our bodies, so often a bleeding wound is stanched by opening a vein and turning the blood another way; and I am persuaded was God's house on these days of humiliation were more moistened with unfeigned tears of penitence, our fields and dwellings would not be soaked and watered with so much blood of the slain, they are the expressions of Isaiah and Ezekiel (Isaiah 34:7; Ezekiel 32:6). Full of awakening terror if you please to read them, and the Lord bring it to your hearts.

And let me entreat you to make use of your tears of Compassion for the miseries of this land, to draw from you tears of humiliation for the sins of this land. How melting are many of us at the reading of some doleful and lamentable relation, which yet can read over and over the sad story of their own and the kingdom's sins without shedding a tear? When so ever then your hearts are affected to express tears of compassion, let them draw out tears of humiliation. Do for this, as those, that coming for water to pump out of order, first cast in water to fetch up water; let your souls take in tears of compassion, that they may be more apt to issue forth tears of humiliation; and surely, I fear we have all cause to be more abundant in these of humiliation, if for no other sin, but this, our want of tears of real compassion for those former miseries the Church has long endured. Remember what fetched tears from that man of God, when he looked on Hazael, it was not for anything at the present done, all runs in the future, "the evil that thou wilt do, their strong holds thou wilt set on fire," (2 Kings 8). And yet could Elisha have thoughts of this in his heart without tears in his eyes, where were then our tears of compassion for Germany and Ireland? In which we have heard all these and worse have been done, their strong holds have been set on fire, their young men have been slain with the sword, their infants have been dashed in pieces, and their women with child ripped up, and many more unheard of cruelties. have we read them with dry eyes? With unrelenting hearts? O labor we to see what great cause we have that our tears of Humiliation should be many, if for no other reason but this, because our tears of compassion have been so few. That you may have both, pray unto the Lord to give unto you tenderness of affection; a tender skin will bleed at the touch of a needle's point, "Be kindly affectioned one toward another with brother love, weep with them that weep," (Romans 12:10, 15). Beg also for broken hearts and wounded souls, a wound in the heart will usually bleed at the eye[36], if the heart is full of bowels of pity within, like full vessels a final touch or shake will make them run over without. Water in the head and heart will have a fountain of tears in the eyes. We, upon such days as these offer (as we think) much to God, offer our lips in prayer, our ears in hearing, our persons and presence in attendance of almost a whole day in this house and service; but would you know why the Lord has not here so fully manifested his acceptance of these offerings, in giving us what we have desired, no, seemed by withholding that, to reject the other; let me tell you, I am afraid, there has been too little of that offered, which I am sure the Lord will not reuse, what David upon his own experience will tell you, "The sacrifices of God are a broken spirit," (Psalm 51:17), sacrifices in the plural for without this there is nothing; and he goes on, "a broken and a contrite heart, O Lord, thou wilt not despise." We of this land may truly complain with the Prophet, with some final variation, "we have seen the breaches of our Kingdom; that they are many," (Isaiah 22:9), breaches in our counsels, in our armies, in our affections, in our estates, and I am persuaded that all our

---

[36] *Fons lachrymal nun est cor empunetuns dolens Cornelia lap in toc. ubi. p. 271.*

breaches yet remain great, because our hearts are so little broken for those great sins that made them; take we heed then lest the withholding our tears of compassion from our brethren's distresses, do not close God's bowels of compassion towards ourselves, and lest our land shedding so few tears for sin, lose not yet much more blood, as the just punishment of our impenitence, and lack of humiliation for sin.

But did Nehemiah rest in his tears for the affliction of the people, and the ruins of Jerusalem? Was his pity only verbal? Like that mercy rejected by the Apostle, when, "to a brother or sister naked and destitute of daily food, one shall say unto him, depart in peace, be you warmed and filled. And yet give them not those things which are needful for the body," (Lamentations 2:15-16). Did they only have a return of good words from Nehemiah? I am sorry to hear of your affliction and reproach, that your walls yet remain broken down, and your gates burnt with fire; but be of good comfort, build your walls, repair your gates, I wish it were in my power to relieve you, and further the work. No, Nehemiah's heart was so fully affected with their miseries and ruins, as it put him upon the use of those means, which if any would prevail for redress of their miseries, and these are two, *fasting and prayer*; such as never failed, when used aright.

For encouragement to the first, I might commend unto you the confidence that God's people in all exigent placed in this, and their comfortable success; that of Jehoshaphat who set the enemies to kill one another (2 Chronicle 20:1); that of Esther changed the heart of the King and reversed a bloody decree near execution (Esther 4 and 5); Ezra more trusted to this for a safe envoy, then to, "a band of the King's soldiers," (Ezra 8. 21-23). Ahab's hypocritical fast put off the judgement to his sons days (1 Kings 21:27-29). Rehaboam and his princes half humiliation (as I may call it) brought, "some deliverance," Shishak King of Egypt had only power to plunder him of his treasures, "not altogether to destroy him," (2 Chronicles 12:7, 9, 13-14), our own comfortable experience since our last fast (blessed be our God) will speak, though we be silent.

And pity it is, that so powerful a remedy, through our miscarriage in it, should lose its power, that our monthly use of it, should make it, like the same medicine often used, uneffectual to us. Give me leave therefore in a few words, to give you the principal heads of the doctrine of fasting, and because in this, I may deliver nothing which is not known to the most here present, these may please, while I speak (it may be) to some for information, to suffer their thoughts to go along with me in a way of examination, remembering that of Christ, "If ye know these things, happy are ye if ye do them," (John 13:17).

The day of our Fast should be observed as a, "holy day, a holy convocation, no work to be done on that day," (Leviticus 23:27-28, 30-32; Numbers 29:7), it is called a Sabbath, and in all respects to be kept with as much, if not more strictness than the Sabbath, sanctified and set apart for holy duties (Joel 1:14), as praying, reading, preaching, hearing, confession of sin, renewing of Covenants, as in that whole chapter of Nehemiah (Nehemiah 9).

The continuance of the Fast, a whole day, "from Evening to Evening," (Leviticus 23. 32). Joshua and the Elders kept it, "till eventide," (Joshua 7:6).

All persons of all ages and conditions to observe it; in Jehoshaphat's fast, "all Judah stood before the Lord with their little ones, their wives, and their children" (2 Chronicles 20:13). In Nineveh's fast, "all from the greatest to the least," (Jonah 3:5).

The outward special duties are 1. Abstinence from food, so far as strength of nature will bear; Ezra in his fast did, "neither eat bread, nor drink water," (Ezra 10:6). In Esther's fast there was a charge, "not to eat nor drink," (Esther 4:16).

Abstaining from marriage comforts, "Let the bridegroom get forth of his chamber, and the bride out of her closet," (Joel 2:16), that of the Apostle makes it clear (1 Corinthians 7:5).

Forbearing better apparel, the Eastern parts used on the days of their fast to lie in sackcloth, in Nehemiah's fast (Nehemiah 9:1), in David's (Psalm 35:13), in that of Nineveh (Jonah 3:5), with other instances that might be added.

Abatement of our ordinary sleep, so that of Esther applied by our Divines, requiring the continuance of the fast, "three days, night and day," (Esther 4:16), as also that of Joel, "lie all night in sackcloth," (Joel 1:13).

And therefore all these, but to further the main duty of the day, the humbling and afflicting of the soul; a duty of such necessity for that day, as, "whatsoever soul it be, that shall not be afflicted in that same day, he shall be cut off from among his people," (Leviticus 23:29). And what will more humble the soul than the serious consideration of its unworthiness to receive pardon of sin, great mercies for the Church in general, for itself in particular, then by its abstinence from all, even the least outward comforts, to profess its unworthiness of any of the least of these. And surely we might by such meditations as these, help to put our souls on the day of our Humiliation into a humbled frame. We come, Lord, to beg this day pardon for our own sins, and the sins of our Nation, reconciliation for ourselves, for Kingdoms, to entreat your Majesty, "to give beauty for ashes, the oil of joy for mourning, the garment of praise for the spirit of heaviness," (Isaiah 61:3), and we acknowledge these in every way so needful for our spiritual life, as food and raiment for our natural body, but, Lord, we profess ourselves most unworthy the least of these, and shall we not be humbled to think, that we are altogether unworthy of any greater favor? I have given you a small hint, your private thoughts may more fully enlarge this.

But are these outward observances, and inward afflicting of the soul sufficient? Do not we hear some in the Prophet complaining? "Wherefore have we fasted, and thou seest not? Wherefore have we afflicted our souls, and thou makest no knowledge?" (Isaiah 58:3). Here you see is both fasting and afflicting, yet no acceptance, what is more then to be done? The Prophet will there tell you, it is a *forsaking of sin* (for I will instance only in that) without which whatsoever is done upon the day of our fast, will neither have power with God, nor bring comfort to ourselves. The Ninevites were very punctual in the out-works of their fast, "The King came down from his throne, put off his robes, clothed himself with sackcloth, there was crying mightily to the Lord, neither man nor beast took any food," (Jonah 3:6), questionless God took notice of all this, yet when the Prophet comes to set down, what moved the Lord not to bring upon them the destruction threatened, he overlooks, as it were all the rest, and fastens upon this, "God saw their works that they turned from their evil way, and so he repented of the evil that he said he would do unto them, and did it not," (Jonah 3:8); and believe it, our fasts will never do that work, for which we keep them, until this is done; now our souls are then truly afflicted for sin, when sin is in our souls, like a thorn in the joint, that will give no rest, until it is out, and surely were our putrefied sores of sin once thoroughly cleansed, I doubt not but the wounds of our land would soon be healed, had the strong medicine, which the Lord has given our nation emptied it of the foulness and fullness of sin, we should err long have cordials of truth and peace, and deliverance ministered unto us; to conclude this, could the Lord see England and Ireland turning from their provoking sins, I doubt not, but England and Ireland should also see God turning from the fierceness of his wrath.

The time hastens me to that other means of Nehemiah's help, his prayer, (another main duty required on this day of Humiliation) and I might be very large in showing what several great encouragements we have to use his help of Prayer in the behalf of the Church, I shall reduce them to three, 1. In respect of God. 2. Of Prayer 3. Of ourselves.

In respect of God, the Lord commands it, no, looks for it, for however God is willing to give, yet it is his will, that we shall ask what we desire to receive, his promises of giving are made upon the condition of asking, as that known place, of Christ, "Ask, and it shall be given you," (Matthew 7:7). The Lord knows what England and Ireland want, and what everyone of us stand in need of, for our particular necessities, and God does not want to give us, his Church, what mercies he sees lacking, but yet he will be sought to give them. Indeed we have cause to bless God, that of his free goodness he often, "presents us with liberal blessings," (Psalm 21:3), (so reads the Geneva) gives many unsought favours, yet it is not safe to stay, until God bestows mercies without asking. many gracious promises are made in the former verses to God's people, but, "thus saith the Lord God, I will yet for this be enquired of by the house of Israel, to do it for them. ," (Ezekiel 36:37), "You have not, [the Apostle says] because you ask not," (James 4:3), and assuredly we want many blessings from God, because the Lord does not have our prayers for them.

The second encouragement is drawn from God's power, "I prayed to the God of Heaven", this assures, that what God's love makes him willing to do, his power enables him to do, when you seek to God in prayer, whatever your necessities be, for soul, for body, for the Church, for yourselves, you do not go to a weak God, that does not have all things to satisfy your desires, but you go to the God of Heaven, that whatsoever is in Heaven, or in the earth, he has it at his command to give.

I proceed to those encouragements that Prayer itself gives to all those that will make use of it, and I hope by God's blessing, they may be some provocations to put us more upon prayer, we all (I hope) desire to help somewhat towards the cause of God, let me tell you, a little to quicken your attention, there is no such way, whereby everyone may help as this of Prayer.

First, it is a help of the largest extent, other helps can go no further than your counsels, persons and purses can reach, but the halo of prayer can extend to the redress of the miseries and distresses of God's people in the farthest parts of the world; David in his meditations traveled through heaven, earth, and the seas, and wherever he went, he found God present (Psalm 119:7, 8, 10); I am sure God's Church and his servants at one time or other have found the like, and their Prayers have in all places met with God, on the land (as more a none) on the sea, as Jonah (Jonah 2:1); the breath of the Churches prayers has raised up such storms in this, as has scattered and distressed invincible navies of their enemies, as England's prayers did that Spanish Armado in '88. They have also stirred up prosperous gales to bring ships for the Churches relief in strait sieges to their, "desired haven," (Psalm 107:30), they did it for late besieged Tredah in Ireland. In a word wherever God is there Prayer can come, and you know God is everywhere, as the Lord himself, "Am I a God at hand, saith the Lord, and not a God afar off? Do not I fill the heavens and earth?" (Jeremiah 23:23, 24).

Secondly, prayer is a speedy help, many places miscarry and are lost, because help comes too late, and many friends would help sooner, if they could tell how sooner to convey help; other helps of men, arms, ammunition, money, *etc*, require time for raising and conveying, whereas this of prayer is a quick, a speedy and present help, our prayers (if such as they should be) are no sooner out of our mouths, no, in our hearts, but they are in Heaven, and no sooner in Heaven, but the benefit of them may be with the distressed Church many thousands of miles distant, Daniel found this, "While I was speaking in prayer, the man Gabriel being caused to fly swiftly, informed me and said, at the beginning of thy supplications the commandment came forth, *etc*," (Daniel 9:21-23).

Thirdly, prayer is an invisible help, many would willingly send relief to friends in distress, if they knew how to convey it with safety and without danger of intercepting, but there lie armies in the way, scouts, ambushments, and many other hazards, now prayer can avoid all these; it can go to God and bring such help from heaven, as the enemies scouts can neither discover nor stop, no ambush can way-lay or surprise it.

Fourthly, there is no such universal help in all extremities as prayer, it is Solomon's *Catholicon*, "whatsoever plague, whatsoever sickness", war, lack of rain, pestilence, famine, cities besieged, enemies prevailing, yet, "if they pray, and make supplications, turn from their sin, when thou afflicted them, then hear thou in Heaven, and forgive, and do, and give to every man according to his ways," (1 Kings 8. 33-39, 44-50); I might single out many encouraging instances, prayer can give victory in doubtful battles, as in Israel's against Amalek, sometime Amalek prevailed, but in the end Moses' hands lifted up in prayer, not Joshua's sword, got the victory (Exodus 17:11). It can recover lost battles, as in the Civil war between the eleven tribes and the Benjamites, after two battles lost, in which were slain forty thousand of the Israelites, prayer in the third obtained the victory (Judges 20:26). Prayer can raise a siege even a dangerous and confident one, as was that of Sennacherib against Jerusalem (Isaiah 37:29, 36). Prayer can turn the plots and wisdom of the greatest State-Politicians into foolishness, and set them onto twist and halter for their own execution; the prayer of David did against Ahithophel (2 Samuel 15:31 and 17:14, 23). I might add many others both out of foreign and our own Histories, the victory against Cadwell and Penda in the time of the Saxons, ascribed to the Prayers of Oswald, the like against Sueno the tyrant, against the Danes[37], I remember an observation I have read of Constantine, that after God had blessed and honored him with many victories, whereas the effigies of other Emperors was engraved on their loins

---

[37] Fox. *Martyr*. Vol. 1. 251, 298, 282.

triumphing, he would be set in a posture of prayer, kneeling, to manifest unto the world, that he attributed all his victories more to his prayers than his sword. What was said of the wicked, "their tongue is a sharp sword, swords are in their lips," (Psalm 57:4), may be truly said of the tongues and lips of God's people in prayer (Psalm 59:17), they are, "as two-edged swords in their hands to execute vengeance," (Psalm 149:6), and surely God's enemies have often found the power of this sword of prayer, and those which are the Lord's people may say of this, when used as it ought , as David once did of that which was Goliath's, "There is none like that, give it me," (1 Samuel 21:9).

To conclude this, such is the prevalent power of prayer, for it is that which God can hear and use; so what is there in prayer that one does not have, or God cannot do? I had almost said, that God cannot do that which the prayers of his servants will not have him do, and I may say it, for the Lord himself has said as much to Moses, "Now therefore let me alone, that my wrath my wax hot," (Exodus 32:10). And I think I hear Moses answering, Lord, *who stops you?* And God replying, *My hands, Moses are tied from executing wrath, while your hands in prayer are lifted up for mercy.*

I come to the last encouragement in reference to ourselves, *prayer is:*

First, a very safe help, many are kept from appearing in the Churches behalf, because afraid of danger, they may hazard the loss of their places of honor or profit, their estates, it may be, their lives. Where Prayer is such a help, that you may use it against the enemy, and for the Church, even when you are in the enemy's quarters, in the enemy's dungeon, and that without all danger, nor can those fetters, that may chain your hands and feet, tie your hearts, your tongues; yet give me leave to tell you, I fear, that such as are not willing to appear openly in the cause of God, when they may do good, will never heartily pray in private for the Churches good.

Secondly, it is an easy help, he that can do nothing else may pray, the French have a Proverb, "He that hath no money in his purse, let him have honey in his mouth," if you have ability, estates enabling you to contribute, or lend towards the maintenance of an army, you may yet contribute your Prayers, and lay out these for the Lord's blessing on the army. You shall hear some of the meaner rank say, were we in such a condition, had we such an estate as these and these men have, we would do this and that, which these and other rich men do not, take heed, we have deceitful hearts, I would have you try them by this, what do you in that condition in which you are, even in this of Prayer? Do you in this do what you can? Are you often on your knees? Earnest with God to pardon the sins of the land? That his cause may prosper, that the expectation of the Churches enemies may be disappointed, that the Lord would give hearts to all those, to whom he has given abilities to lay out their utmost for the furtherance of God's work? Certainly if you are lacking in this, let me tell you, if you had greater estates you would not do much, I cannot think, that he which will not use his tongue, will to any purpose use his hands or purse.

Thirdly, it is a lasting help, your strength, your estate may fail, you may be many ways disabled from yielding that help in other ways, which you desire, nothing can disable you from this, while you have a heart you may pray.

Lastly, in what place so ever you are, you may by your Prayers help the Church, "I will that men pray everywhere," (1 Timothy 2:8; Ephesians 6:18), said the Apostle; those Christians which have put on them that piece of armour, prayer, may use it in their beds, in their chambers, in their shops, in their most private closets; in a word, that soldier, which fights for the Church with his Prayers, (and all may be such) wherever he is, he still keeps file, he cannot in any place be out of rank.

Well then, seeing prayer is of such excellence use, and that whereby everyone may help the Church, let me speak to all of this, as in the Prophet one once did of that Cluster, "Destroy it not, for there is a blessing in it," (Isaiah 65:8), O do not destroy it by your prayers, by not using them aright, it is a

Cluster from where may be pressed many sweet and comfortable blessings, take we heed then, lest by our not using them as we should they prove useless to us, and to the Churches cause for which we use them; the poorest and meanest amongst you may be instruments by this of great mercies to the people of God, and to your own souls, be careful then whatever you do, not to destroy your prayers by your ill usage of them. To help you in this, give me leave to prescribe some few short and plain directions for the right use of prayer, and for your better improvement of this so excellent a help, to the best advancement of the cause of God.

First, Prayer that would prevail with God, must go up with a humble and sorrowful confession of sins, and well-grounded resolution to forsake them, for certainly he that prays today, and returns to his former sins tomorrow, unprays his prayers, and they which fast and confess their sins today, and fall to the practice of them tomorrow, though they may seem too fast to God today, yet indeed they feast the devil tomorrow; the Lord looks for at our hands, not alone the words of prayer, but (as I may call them) the works of prayer, and though on this day, "We may cause our voice to be heard on high," (Isaiah 58:4), yet not casting off our iniquities, our works of sin will outcry our words of prayer. Let everyone then, I beseech you, search into his own soul, and find out the sins he stands guilty of, and whenever he goes to prayer, to preface to his soul with that of the Psalmist, "If I regard iniquity in my heat, the Lord will not hear me," (Psalm 66:18); and do not forget that of the Apostle, "I will that men pray everywhere lifting up pure hands," (1 Timothy 2:8), for undoubtedly, if God sees impurity in our hands, we shall find little prevalence in our prayers (Isaiah 1:15).

Prayer must go up with fervency, heat and ardency of affection, "Let my prayer come before thee as incense," (Psalm 141:2), said the Psalmist; and this never went up without fire, you know who said it, and upon what occasion, "The effectual fervent prayer of a righteous man availeth much," (James 5:16), effectual and fervent joined, to teach us, that our prayers, the more fervent they are, are always the more effectual, the Geneva reads, "The prayer of a righteous man availeth much if it be fervent." The more fervency, the more prevalency in our prayers. The soldiers of this City are commended for good firemen, that there is powder and shot in their muskets will do no execution unless they fire well. O that which are this day fighting without prayers, would labor for this fervency in our prayers, if they be nothing else but words, they are but as the powder and shot in a pistol, if there is no fire, no fervency of spirit, they will never go off, so as either to reach Heaven, or the Churches enemies. Of all the four elements, that of fire is nearest Heaven, the more fire in anything, the higher it ascends heavenward; cold sluggish prayers have so much earth in them, that like the Grasshopper, if they mount a little upward, they are presently down again, fall short of heaven; of all warlike engines your grenading fireworks are most deadly, of all prayers, those that have the most fire, the most fervency, are the most killing.

A third prerequisite in prayer is constancy and perseverance. Importunity which is often offensive to man is always pleasing to God, it was commended by Christ in those two parables of the friend at midnight (Luke 11:5, 8), and the widow with the unjust Judge (Luke 18:1, 5). We may not say of our approaches to God, as Solomon of our neighbor, "withdraw thy foot from thy neighbor's house"(Proverbs 25:17), or as in the margin it says, "Let thy foot be seldom in thy neighbor's house, lest he be weary of thee and hate thee;" no the oftener with God in his house, in our own houses, the more welcome, the Lord will not say, here is an unreasonable man and woman, I can never be rid of them, never at rest for them. They are still following me, praying, and crying, and seeking with everyday a new suit, they came to me the other day for power against oaths, I gave it to them; they came the next for strength against uncleanness, I heard them; they came again for power against pride, stability to subdue sinful passions, I did not deny, *etc.*, and so what grace they lack, they come to me for it, they asked a humbled and broken heart, I gave it to them; a tender conscience, they have it; love of the word and helps to profit by it, I bestowed it, yet still they are following me, they cannot read a Chapter, sing a Psalm, hear a Sermon, not receive food, undertake any business, but I am sought unto for a blessing. O no, God will never cast it into your teeth, that you may rest satisfied with what he has done for you, and trouble him no further, that you come too often; we shall indeed hear God complaining, "thou hast wearied me with thine iniquities," (Isaiah 43:24); but never, that he was wearied with the prayers of his people, when such as they ought, no suitors so welcome to God, as those which are most importunate, God's people may be, "upbraided with their unbelief, and hardness of heart," (Mark 16:14), never with their too often praying, hear the Apostle, "The Lord giveth liberally to all, and upbraideth not," (James 1:5). Let me then speak to all those, whose spirits are ready to fail, and their hearts near sinking, because after many prayers they have not what they desire, that if they will with Jacob hold God to it, "not let him go except he bless," (Genesis 32:26), such is the goodness of God, they, "that asking according to his will," (1 John 5:14), will take *no no*, shall have *no no*, but may be assured, that what they strive by earnestness and holy importunity, to rest (as it were) out of God's hands, he will at length in his own good time give into their bosoms. The Canaanitish woman found it, who fastening the more upon Christ, by all those means by which he seemed to beat her off, had at length, the utmost, if not more then she sought, "Be it unto thee even as thou wilt," (Matthew 15:28).

In the last place, consider to whom Nehemiah goes in prayer, it is to the God of heaven, "I prayed before the God of Heaven." I have told you, that the main business he went about, was that he might find mercy in the sight of the King, so the close of the last verse of this chapter will tell you, and all the words following, until we come to that, are a continued prayer for this. He knew it was in the king's power to give liberty and assistance, for relief of the people's miseries, and the repair of Jerusalem's ruins, that if there was a probable way on earth to do it, it must be done by the King, yet observe his first step was Heavenward. He had a place of great trust and favour with the King, so he says of himself, "I was the King's cupbearer," (Nehemiah 1:21), or as others, "Pragustator", his taster, which might have encouraged him first to make known unto the King the condition of the People and City, and his own heaviness of heart for their affliction and decays, but he dares not rely on that, therefore he begins with God, "and prayed before the God of Heaven."

I know the desire of all our souls has long been and is, that (if God please) our Parliament, and those which adhere to it, and the cause for God, Religion and lawful liberties and privileges, which they desire to preserve might find grace and mercy in the sight of our King, we learn from Nehemiah's practice, what is the likeliest way to have our desires in this satisfied. In the following chapter you shall hear the King asking Nehemiah, "Why is thy countenance sad? For what dost thou make request?" (Nehemiah 2:3, 4). What would you have me do? One would think here was encouragement enough to put him upon the present, making known all his desires to the King, yet he first goes to God, "So I prayed to the God of Heaven, and I said unto the King," (Nehemiah 2:4, 5). He had no hope that his petition would find acceptance with man, which had not been first presented unto God. you shall hear the like of old Jacob in that great famine of Canaan, his sons, at their first sending into Egypt, found a great deal of rough and hard both words and deeds from Joseph the governor, Simeon was left in prison behind them in Egypt, and they must not return for further provision into Egypt, except they brought Benjamin with them, their good aged father was now in a wonderful strait, the famine increased, their former corn eaten up, hear Jacob lamenting, "Me have you bereaved of my children, Joseph is not, and Simeon is not, and ye will take Benjamin away, all these things are against me," (Genesis 42:36), but what was Jacob's way for help in this strait? He had no hope of relief, but in the Governor's favour, and what course did he take to win it? He does not omit other means, "If it must needs be so now, do this. Take of the best fruits in the land in your vessels, and carry down the man a present,"

(Genesis 43:11), but did Jacob trust in this, or the return of double money in their sacks, and the sending of Benjamin with them? Which at last was all that Jacob desired. No, Jacob rested in none of these. He had a former comfortable experience, which might help to lessen him in this, it was not the present he sent to Esau, but the prayer he put up to God, which gave him favour in the sight of Esau (Genesis 32:9-11, 28), it is this that he now trusts unto, "God Almighty give you mercies before the man," (Genesis 43:14), and it was this that wrought it. and certainly. Let us rest assured, there is no such prevailing way to regain the heart of our King, (which should have a chief place in the petitions of his day) as to beg it of God by Prayer.

That known place of Solomon gives sufficient ground for this, "The heart of the King is in the hand of the Lord, as the rivers of waters, he turneth it whither so ever he will," (Proverbs 21:1). I might be large in giving, though but a short touch upon the several translations and Interpretations of those words [*rivers of waters*] every one of which may commend some useful meditation; the Italian reads small springs, *Sanctes Pagninus* and *Vatablus rivuli*, small prils,[38] alluding to the custom of those which use to draw small springs, or brooks over dry and barren soils, which they easily turn with a hand plough,

---

[38] Deodate.

which way they please, so easily is the heart of the King inclined this or that way, as seems good to the Lord, instances Ahaseurus (Esther 3:11 and 8:8), Darius, (Daniel 1:6-9, 26).

The *Septuagint, impetus aque*[39], the violence of waters, or violent waters, so the verb coming of this in the New Testament is translated running or rushing violently (Matthew 8:32; Acts 19:29), implying, that let the King's heart be set never so violently on this or that resolution, yet, "the Lord that sitteth and ruleth on the floods," (Psalm 29:10), that can calm the greatest tempest, is able at his pleasure to quiet the most violent spirits of Princes. And some from here refer it to the ebbing and flowing of the sea, to assure, that God, "who hath set bars and doors to the sea, and said, Here shalt thou come, and no further, and here shall thy proud sea, and when the waves thereof arise, thou stillest them," (Job 38:10-11; Psalm 89:9), the same God has set the counsels and power of Kings their bounds and limits, which they shall not pass, and can easily, and if he please, suddenly calm their rage. What a full and comfortable evidence hereof is that of Nebuchadnezzar's rage and fury against Shadrach, Meshach, and Abednego, verse 13, full of fury, verse 19, yet see how quickly God calmed him, verse 26-29, the place is worth your reading, and observation; you shall see how suddenly Nebudchanezzar's blaspheming God, verse 15, turned into,

---

[39] *Motus violentus & imperousus*, St. Ph. Psalm 29:10.

"his blessing God", Verse 28, his, "decree for worshipping the golden image", verse 10, changed into a decree for the honor of the true God, verse 29, "his rage and fury against Shadrach, Meshach and Abednego", verse 15, converted, "into his promoting them", verse 30 (Daniel 3:13-14, 19-20).

The vulgar Latin reads *divisiones aquarum*, the divisions of waters, referring this either to the clouds of those waters above, "the bottles of Heaven," (Job 38:37), which the Lord is pleased to empty on this place, and not on that, as in the Prophet (Amos 4:7). Or to the river Nilus, whose overflowing sometimes fruitful, sometimes hurtful, so the Lord inclines the hearts of Kings to the good of his people, according to that of the Psalmist concerning a good King, "He shall come down like rain upon the mown grass, as showers that water the earth," (Psalm 72:6). Another time to the hurt of their people, suffering them to be like the waters of Marah full of bitterness (Exodus 15:23), and which is worse, like the waters in, "the rivers of Egypt turned into blood", insomuch, "as there was blood throughout all the land of Egypt," (Exodus 7:20, 21). Others following the vulgar refer these divisions of water, to the Lord's dividing the Red Sea, that when Pharaoh and his servants, repenting of that liberty they had given to Israel for their passage out of Egypt, pursued them with their whole strength. as the Lord in that great strait of his people, made a division of the waters in the sea for their safe passage, but caused them to return upon and drown Pharaoh and all his forces; so the Lord can turn the counsels and pursuits of such Kings, that set themselves against God and his people, as to the good of his people, so to the ruin of themselves and their adherents; but in this the Lord is merciful to our king for his safety, and if nothing will calm the rage of the sons of Belial, that then all the storms and waves which their malice and fury has raised may return on their own heads, and overwhelm themselves.

To close all with some short *application*, give me leave to express my thoughts, what is the best and likeliest way to have that mercy which Nehemiah here sought, that we might at the length find favour in the sight of our King. You have heard that the heart of the King is in the Lord's hand, and if ever we have it to our comfort, we must have it from there. Now a prevailing way for this with God is; let the Lord in our prayers for the King's heart, see in us Nehemiah's spirit. He was all for the public, as will appear in several verses of the second Chapter, not one for his own particular (Nehemiah 2:3, 5, 7-8); let the Lord then see that our desires for the return of our King are for the general good of Church and State, that God's cause, Reformation may be advanced, that we may behold Jerusalem in its beauty, Religion in its power and purity, "Many [*Solomon says*] seek the ruler's favour," (Proverbs 29:26), but for what? Surely mostly for that of Saul, "He will give every one of you fields and vineyards, and make you all captains of thousands, and captains of hundreds," (1 Samuel 22:7). Are not too many of our hearts too much after such as these? So we may fit under our own vine, we little care what becomes of God's vineyard, let the wild boar makes what spoil and havoc he will in this. It troubles us little, so we can keep him out of our own; Jerome reports of Nebridius[40] the Empress sister's son, a great courtier, and in special favour with Princes, that he never put up any suit but for others, chiefly the poor, and such as were in distress, insomuch as Princes usually granted his petitions; upon this ground, what we give unto him, we give to many; certainly it would much work with God, to give us our King's favour, if he did see, that we would improve it for common good, especially for Religion, when we not care much how it goes with us in our particular, so that we may be safe and prosper. David is an excellent pattern, when things were at the worst, as in several verses (2 Samuel 15:12, 14, 23), yet what was the chiefest of David's care, for himself, or for his own safety? No, he so much looked to the public, the safety of the Ark, which was Israel's glory saying in that extremity of his Zadok, "Carry back the Ark of God into the City," (1 Samuel 4:22), let that be safe, and for myself, and mine own safety, I leave that to God, "If I shall

---

[40] Hieron. Ad Salvinam de viduitate servanda.

find favour in the eyes of the Lord, he will bring me again, and show me both it, and his habitation. But if he says, I have no delight in thee, behold, here am I, let him do to me, as seemeth good unto him," (1 Samuel 15:25, 26).

That God may be pleased to give us our King's heart, let us in truth and sincerity give God our hearts, be cordial in his cause, look chiefly at his glory, many in these times may be for the common good, but it is for such things, as if we have them by means of our King's favour and presence, we cannot truly say, it is that favour which God gives. And I am persuaded the Lord has justly withheld our King from us, because in our desires for his return, we have too little looked to God, to Religion, too much unto other things. What is the common voice? Had we the Court among us, our full Parliament, our usual terms, how would all professions be gainers, our former trading go forward, and profits come in? I must in this leave everyone to the scrutiny of his own heart, and to that God, who is the searcher of all hearts, he knows in this what our desires are, and what we look at in our desires, certainly had the Lord and his cause more reality in our hearts, we should find more interest in the heart of our King.

We must we go to God for all favour that we should have from our King, such indeed as will bring comfort with it, and that because the King's heart is in God's hand, let us not seek to take it there by any indirect or unwarrantable way, let us be sure, that what is given us by our King, is given in God's way, and by such means, as we know the Lord will own; let us not desire that favour from our King, which we cannot truly say, we received from God's hand and which we know cannot stand with God's honor to give. Let then, I beseech you, in the Name of our God (whom this concerns) be careful that no Propositions for Peace be tendered to our King, but such as first in your serious thoughts have been presented to Christ, "the Prince of Peace," (Isaiah 9:6) find out first the mind of Christ, before your minds are made known to the King, for undoubtedly there can be no comfortable assurance of establishing that peace on earth, which has not also sanction in Heaven.

We are all for peace, we daily pray for it, our Armies fight for it, yet not for peace on any terms, not a peace dishonorable to God, but for such a peace, as may best further and keep our peace with God (and I doubt not but the desires of all our worthy Patriots souls are for this). And here give me leave to mind you of Appius Clandim, his carriage in the Treaty for Peace between Pyrrhus and the Romans[41], Pyrrhus fought three battles against the Romans, in the first two he got the victory, but with such great loss of his men in both, that it was said of him for the first, he might *gloriari, non gander,*

---

[41] Plutarch. *Pyrrhus.*

brag of his victory, not rejoice; for the second himself was heard to say, that if he got such another victory, he was undone; after the first, Overtures were made by *iniae, Pyrrhus'* Ambassador in the Senate for Peace, and many were apt to incline into it, as disheartened by *Pyrrhus'* late victory, and fear of a speedy second attempt, of which *appius Claudius* having notice, being blind, very aged, and who had devoted himself wholly into privacy. Yet the noise of peace with *Pyrrhus* so worked with him, as he caused himself to be carried in his couch to the Senate house, and presently breaks out, *Worthy and noble Patriots and Senators of Rome, I have here with some grief endured the loss of my fight, but now that I hear your consultations and inclinations to decree a Peace so unworthy and dishonorable to the glory and renown of this City of Rome, with Pyrrhus your professed enemy, it now most troubles me, that I am only blind, and not also deaf, that mine ears might not hear so great an infamy and reproach to Rome.* I know unto whom in this I speak. I shall leave the application to their own thoughts.

Lastly, will not the Lord be pleased to give us the favour of our King in a lawful and warrantable way? Cannot we yet obtain that from him, which we may with confidence and comfort say, the Lord had given? Let this be the supporting cordial of God's people, that though they cannot have the King's heart, yet God has it in his hand, and why should we seek to take it out of the Lord's hand, otherwise then who will give it, can it be anywhere better? Has anyone any more wisdom than God, to guide and steer it? Can it be with any that bears more truth and tenderness of affection to the Church than God does? Shall it not satisfy, that there is not a thought in the heart of any King, but what is disposed of by the Lord? Does not that of Solomon hold true even of Kings? "The preparations of the heart of man, and the answer of the tongue is from the Lord," (Proverbs 16:1). As also, that in a following Chapter, "There are many devices in a man's heart, nevertheless the counsel of the Lord shall stand," (Proverbs 19:21). assuredly, we may say of all the Kings on earth, as Balaam once said of himself, they, "cannot do either good or bad of their own mind," (Numbers 24:13), but what the Lord puts into their hearts and hands. It will give us a great deal of satisfaction, when we hear of a powerful man, one that may do us much hurt, and that we know bears us no great good will, yet we are assured, that we have a fast friend, which has his heart and hands in his power, and can turn and wind it (as we say) at his pleasure, and we are confident, that he neither will nor can do anything against us but what our trusty faithful friend will give way unto. This is the Church's condition, and in this its happiness, and here may it keep up the spirits of God's people. However sons of Belial, and of violence have had on us, and still keep our King's person, or may be something stopping his hand, yet God still keeps his heart in the power of his hands, to dispose of it, as his love and wisdom sees it expedient. In this let us be content that it may rest, until the Lord is pleased in his own way, and his own time to give it to the prayers of his people, and those other means which the Lord shall please to own and further.

I dare lead you no further then to the *Throne of Grace*, to crave a Blessing upon what the Lord has given you attention and patience to hear, and to my weakness, strength to deliver. *Amen.*

*FINIS*

www.ingramcontent.com/pod-product-compliance
Lightning Source LLC
Chambersburg PA
CBHW031957080426
42735CB00007B/432